RICHARD
BACH

FROM THE AUTHOR OF THE BESTSELLER
JONATHAN LIVINGSTON SEAGULL

TRAVELS
WITH *Puff*

A Gentle Game of Life and Death

Also by Richard Bach

Stranger to the Ground
Biplane
Nothing by Chance
Flying: The Aviation Trilogy (single volume)
Jonathan Livingston Seagull
A Gift of Wings
There's No Such Place as Far Away
Illusions: The Adventures of a Reluctant Messiah
The Bridge Across Forever
One
Running from Safety
Out of My Mind: The Discovery of Saunders-Vixen
Messiah's Handbook: Reminders for the Advanced Soul
Hypnotizing Maria
Thank Your Wicked Parents

The Ferret Chronicles

Rescue Ferrets at Sea
Air Ferrets Aloft
Writer Ferrets: Chasing the Muse
Rancher Ferrets on the Range
The Last War: Detective Ferrets and the Case of the Golden Deed
Curious Lives: Adventures from the Ferret Chronicles (single volume)

Travels with *Puff*
A Gentle Game of Life and Death

by Richard Bach

Photos *by* Dan Nickens

Copyright © 2013 by Richard Bach
Photographs Copyright © 2013 by Dan Nickens

Nice Tiger
5190 Neil Road, Suite 430
Reno NV 89502
publisher@nicetiger.com
www.nicetiger.com

Cover design by Jack Hovenier
Interior design and composition by Rick Soldin

Library of Congress Cataloging-in-Publication Data available.

ISBN: 978-1-937777-03-6

Contents

Travels with *Puff*

In Case You Won't Believe This

I didn't know it as I wrote, but *Travels with Puff* turned out to be a story hummed about the theme-song for my brief stay on this planet. Same song's shared by I don't know how many hundreds of millions: What is it to become free, and how do I express my freedom to choose my own life, every day?

The mavericks among us, our wanderers, our explorers, they hand us examples all the time. Willing to give up convention, willing to cast off from visible security for the invisible, or for no security at all? "Hi-ho, adventurers, fellow mavericks, steer this way!"

Not me. I'm no maverick. My only claim to mavericity is twofold: 1) I do not own a tie, and 2) I have never worn a tuxedo. Further, stubborn defiance, I intend never to do either, for so long as I may live. Not claim enough to become an Alpha Maverick, I'm somewhere down the list among the Lambdas, or the Upsilons.

For this reason, some suspect that I may bend the truth, in my books, play fast with it, if not loose.

I have no smallest doubt that this story would be subject to those claims, as well, you'd think I made it up. I knew before ever I met Mister Toad, or even Puff herself, that others would doubt these meetings really happened, doubt that anything on these pages was more than the idle writer rising an inch from his feather-pillows to pen his imaginings.

Enter my humble cell-phone camera for the first sketchy evidence: photographs. Next enter Dan Nickens, his matching spirit, his own experimental seaplane, sister to Puff, and his unmatched one-of-a-kind Canon EOS 5D Series II Full Frame CMOS Digital Single Lens Reflex Compact Body Super-Camera, the better to fasten upon the truth of each word, every day's adventure which you may very well be about to read.

Destiny brought us together for this flight, and for love of you, dear reader, to prove once and always that every event, every idea upon the following pages or upon your high-tech visi-screen pseudopage is every single one of them true, and here be the photographs to prove it!

Not wild adventure, through this volume, but gentle, of the sort that anyone can assay, with near certainty; no requests for dying along the way which can't be declined.

A few years ago, someone asked me by way of their T-shirt, "Got Freedom?"

Here's, a bit delayed and by way of two small seaplanes and a continent ten thousand horizons wide, my answer.

—**Richard Bach**

Chapter 1

The Encounter

Remember *The Wind in the Willows?*

In that story, do you recall Mister Toad, the enthusiastic Lord of Toad Hall? You didn't find him ... eccentric, did you?

Neither did I.

His first sight of a Motor-Car, and his fascination with the machine, you wouldn't call that "obsession," would you?

Neither would I.

Came the day, when Toad saw an Aero-Plane, for which he dropped the Motor-Car like an old jam-pot, it was his natural wish to taste the freedom that is flight above the earth, was it not?

No more than that.

Toad said it better than ever I could: "There's no freedom without independence, my friends. No freedom without shattering the chains of Someone Else pushing, forcing, deciding my life against my will!"

He stood in the great Hall, stood before his friends Ratty and Mole and Badger and me: "Freedom, I say! Freedom's living not as someone says I must, but living true to my unchained spirit!"

"Hear! Hear!" We four shouted agreement, pounded the table with our open paws, fine silverware set a-rattling.

1

Toad, he spoke my truth. When we've won independence at last, what shall we do with the freedom it brings—live by the rules of others? There's naught more independent than a flying machine, I say, naught more free than an Aero-Plane, one so near the twin of Toad's that he could fly it blindfold!

We're not talking Then, or Long Ago, we're talking Now!

Being thus persuaded yesterday, I bought an Aero-Plane.

CHAPTER 2

The Advertisement

2008 SEAREY 912S 73 T.T.A.E. • FOR SALE TO GOOD HOME • This is a Searey 'Classic' that has been fitted with a few Searey LSX upgrades: Vortex Generators, Strut Plates, Tail Post Strap and LSX Bulkhead Upgrade. Carbon 'C' Hull, Rotax 912ULS 100 HP Engine, Electric Gear, Electric Flaps, Hydraulic Brakes w/ Hegar 6.00 x 6 Rims, 3 Blade Ivo Prop, 26 Gallon Fuel Tank, 40 Amp External Alternator, Oil Cooler, Whelen Navs / Strobes. • Contact Jim Ratte— RECREATIONAL MOBILITY, Broker—located Malabar, FL USA • Telephone: 321-253-9434; http://www. seareyspecialist.com.

All those technical words mean something to me, as they ought after a lifetime messing around with air-craft. This machine, so like Toad's, it occurred to me ... well, *I'm* a good home!

I called Jim Ratte (pronounced "Ratty," as Toad's loyal friend) at 321-253-9434 and he answered hello and I said, "*I'm* a good home!"

Isn't she a sweet little thing? She's a flying-boat, of course: flies through air, lands on earth, floats on water. Only one thing about such an airplane you've got to remember: Land on land, put the wheels down. Land on water, bring the wheels up. Any amphibian airplane, dare you touch on a lake or a river with the wheels down, there's this monster splash and you do your cursing and self-recriminations mostly underwater. I'm pretty good about checking wheels up for water landings, though, I can handle that.

There's one minor challenge: my new delight lives in a hangar in Florida, twenty-eight hundred miles, as crows fly, from my home in Washington State. I'll be off, therefore, clean across the continent, to fly my airplane thirty-four hundred miles home, as it is not a crow and there's still winter in the mountains, snows and winds to be avoided like midnight zombies by little airplanes.

Here's a perfect example of Thought, all drums and cymbals, changing my everyday world of three dimensions, the kid from my past aglow with visions, bursting into my life, dragging me into his passions once more: *Adventure! Romance! Life on the High Frontier!*

If you've read *The Ferret Chronicles*, does that cry sound familiar? Can you hear the stir in the ferret world … Budgeron and Strobe and Cheyenne, Stormy and Bethany? Particularly in Bethany's, since should we qualify, the little seaplane and I may have a chance to fly with the Ferret Rescue Service at FRS Base Maytime, not so far from our home. With the SeaRey, we could fly over Bethany's Ferret Rescue Boat: *J-101 Resolute*, me scouting above on her mission to save small animals in danger at sea.

I'll learn to fly the machine from an instructor, get comfortable flying it, then spend the next few weeks flying it home. Who knows? Could be another pilot in her or his own plane might join me!

I'll practice, first-person everyday, my brand of the freedom we've all been given, to live as we choose. The SeaRey can go nearly anywhere, practically anywhen. That's all the freedom I ask, to take her there as I wish.

If I've learned one lesson in all my days, it's this: *We each decide our chessboard and our playground, each of us chooses the stage on which we'll play.*

I'll take the sky. Is there anyone but myself, who can keep me from going there, from living as I please? Who's to stop me? My guess is nobody.

I plan to find if that's true.

CHAPTER 3

From Frail Thought into The World of Appearances

y time's still a bit off kilter after the long airline flight to pre-dawn Orlando, but I'm recovering now in Florida. Off the jetliner, I drove at once from the big Orlando airport to the little one in Valkaria, to the SeaRey's hangar on the Atlantic coast.

First, she's called Three Four Six Papa Echo.

Second, she's a beautiful little seaplane.

Third, I am just nutty about her.

The feeling, however, isn't mutual.

First touch, my fingers to her silken fiberglass fuselage. Hallo, little airplane, I thought, by way of courteous introduction.

No answer, but an odd sense, shrinking back:

Don't touch me. Go away!

"Jim?" I said to the man who built her, "is there a problem?"

"You can tell, can't you?" he said.

"Never had that feeling before, an airplane's scared of me!"

He stroked her wing as he'd stroke the flank of a frightened pony. "Her first owner landed her wheels-down in the water."

I winced.

"She was flying light, though, and the wind was strong, so she hit going slow. She wasn't destroyed. She was built back to new."

"You said first owner. There was a second?"

He nodded, his hand still gently on her wing: it's OK, little one, it's OK ..."The second owner, he was pretty sure he didn't need a checkout. He knew he could fly her just fine."

He was quiet, remembering.

"And that turned out not to be quite true?"

"Not quite. She hit a tree after liftoff, her left wing. Hit fairly hard. We built her a new wing, back to new again. Owner doesn't care for the airplane, now, doesn't want her any more."

The last two times new owners said hello, I thought, was just before they crashed her. She's scared of her third owner? No wonder!

Hours talking about the SeaRey, talking while Jim finished installing the heated carburetors I wanted her to have, hours then just sitting quiet in her cockpit, getting used to the feel of it, where the switches and dials, what the view must be, in the air. Then more talk with my instructor, and out we went to fly.

No need for technical details, enough to say I welcomed the training in the little airplane, hours that first day.

Never did it occur to me that I was doing a mad thing, buying an experimental amateur-built airplane. If I learn who she is, if I learn to fly her well, could we be friends, could we fly not clenched-teeth separate, but could we some day lift into that bright freedom I saw, fly there together, each of us glad for the other?

If I've learned one lesson in all my days, it's this: *Every joyful hope is possible, one way or another, when we hold the delight and the love of it in our heart.*

CHAPTER 4

The Curve
of Learning

B ack in my hotel room now, and the little SeaRey safe in her hangar, so you know the airplane and I survived the second day of my checkout.

How strange, to watch my inner self learning, getting used to what seemed odd and uncomfortable only yesterday. She's like no airplane I've flown, quick and light in the air, a constant swirl of new to learn.

She's small, as low to the ground as a lawn-chair on the runway, her pilot seat reclining instead of upright, the engine throttle to my right hand instead of the left, electric switches to run the landing gear and flaps, instead of familiar levers and handles.

Oddly enough, she isn't easy to fly well ... sensitive as a thistledown, she didn't respond well to a mind grown used to heavier airplanes. My first takeoffs were awkward and erratic, the landings as bad or worse (flyers call them "controlled crashes"). The bright side? She proved she was built strong enough to stand a student pilot.

Practice, and landings improved, became smoother, but happy with them I am not, nor happy with myself. The airplane needs to be flown with a surgeon's touch, and I've been flying her like a butcher.

My instructor was breathing easier today. I noticed, flying down yet another approach to land, that he didn't seem to think his life was in quite so much danger as it was yesterday, those first awful touchdowns. He was alert as a cat, of course, ready to grab the controls if I lost it completely, if I somehow rolled us inverted after a landing-bounce and screamed, "YOU'VE GOT IT!" but I had the sense that he felt it was less likely today that such a thing could happen. Way too slowly was I beginning to get the feel of her:

to lighten up, Richard, for God's sake, adapt to her instead of forcing her to adapt to you. She's built strong, but she's a light light *light* airplane!

Nearly all practice, learning a new amphibian seaplane, is landing practice, whether it's ground or water. That's because most machines are easy to handle in the air, once one gets used to them. Climbs and glides and turns and stalls, it takes only minutes to find here's how she flies these things: here's how her wing stalls, here's normal for her turns, her climbs, her glides.

The challenge in most flying, and what pilots most enjoy (or yesterday, in my case, struggle with), is landing: every one is different. The wind changes, the airplane's a little lighter or heavier than it was last landing, other aircraft join or leave the traffic pattern, eagles and gulls and buzzards drift in and out, choices vary second to second.

He's a low-key instructor, lets me learn at my own speed, doesn't carry on about explaining things in the air. He's listening carefully, though, when I say my checklists. "This is going to be a WATER landing. Left wheel's UP, tailwheel's UP, right wheel's UP, the wheels indicate UP for a WATER landing ..." He wants to hear this because there are videos anyone can find, that show how tall a splash it makes, wheels-down in the water, just before the airplane that was there a second ago floats now serenely upside down on the blue.

I follow that with, "Boost pump's ON, flaps are twenty, for a WATER landing." So this morning we flew a square pattern around a wilderness lake (there are around a million of these in central Florida), I pulled the power back to idle and we whispered down the last turn into the wind, the surface of the water big and getting bigger fast.

He's the only instructor I know who uses the term "ground rush" for the landing approach, the SeaRey the only airplane that gives that feeling. The words he borrowed from skydiving, to describe those last seconds of a fall when all of a sudden one realizes that the ground is approaching one's body at extremely high speed. In the 'Rey we have a choice that skydivers don't have, that is, we can have the joy of watching ground-rush without the pesky requirement of dying, one second later. We accomplish this by easing back on the control stick, the wavelets on the water blurring twelve inches beneath us, now six inches, now the quick-ruffling hiss of her carbon-fiber hull touching water.

This morning we did some water landings as touch-and-go (seaplane pilots call it "splash and dash"), in which I brought the power up again after we touched the waves. The power kept us skimming the lake, a speedboat for a few seconds, then launching back into the sky. Then some landings to a full stop, after which we floated like a fishing-boat on the surface. Then full power once more, spray flying out from under the hull, all snow on velvet blue. Climb into the air and turn back to look, there's our wake on the water, but the boat's gone! (Because we're the boat, and we're in the sky, now.)

Do you get the idea of what fun this is? Yes it takes training, and yes it's difficult and frustrating at first, the airplane so sensitive to its controls, to a wrong touch. Then we learn it and we say, "How could I ever have found this hard to do? It's so easy, flying a SeaRey!" Take off from anywhere, land anywhere, go anywhere you want. There's Toad's kind of freedom, and mine, too.

We did that over and over and over, three flights today of nothing but takeoffs and landings on the water, takeoffs and landings on the land. Slowly I'm learning to become part of the airplane myself, my spirit settling down in this new body, flexing its wings ... "Ah yes ... with this body I can FLY!"

Meanwhile she's silent, scared, waiting, wincing at my early duck-landing-on-ice slides and landing bounces.

Please don't crash me again.

CHAPTER 5

Alone At Last

my instructor offered to fly yet one more training flight with me this morning, but I was anxious to get out on my own, to fly the SeaRey to my place in central Florida, get some rest, then practice quietly, just the plane and me.

"Not to worry, " I said, "you've taught me well and I am grateful. I'll show you a perfect takeoff and departure and hope to see you soon!"

"You know what to remember," he said.

"Gear Flaps Boost-pump!"

"You got it."

So saying, I stuffed my baggage into the various compartments, softcase on the passenger seat, strapped it down. I climbed into the airplane, taxied to the runway and proceeded to make the worst takeoff of my entire flying career.

If ever you've seen the Drunken Pilot Act at an airshow, you've seen my takeoff this morning. The poor little 'Rey staggered into the air, eyes big as dinner plates,

Please not again! What have I done to deserve this man at my controls?

What happened is that I was thinking about other things instead of holding the control stick back to keep the tailwheel on the ground for a while, instead of coming in with right rudder for takeoff ... in short, I managed to be absent while the airplane did her terrified best to take off by herself as I went missing.

11

For the next fifty miles I cursed myself as best I could (I am not strong on cursing), and more important, vowed to begin thinking about every take-off before releasing brakes, instead of pushing the throttle full power and drifting off to dreamland.

Finally I laughed at myself. "OK, guy. Lesson learned. You can let up on me now."

Meanwhile (for I was absent from flying while cursing) the little plane found her way up to an altitude of 1,500 feet on her own, settled down on course and patiently waited for me to notice. When I did, Oh, my!

No longer moving swiftly through my memorized checklists: Pre-Takeoff to Takeoff to Climb to Cruise to Pre-Landing to triple-check the wheels set for landing to Go-Around to Climb to Cruise, I noticed: the world is glorious, down there!

I slid the clear-glass hatch open, put my elbow on the sill as I did when I drove my first automobile, wind racing by. Open cockpit again, as I haven't flown since one summer in the Fleet biplane, Donald Shimoda's Travel Air floating alongside.

The visibility in this aircraft is outstanding except for behind, which is not where the 'Rey is headed, anyway. Forward and to the sides it's to make one laugh, and with the cockpit open one's laugh is whisked by the wind over miles unrolling below.

The little plane had if not forgotten at least forgiven my awful takeoff. I sensed she was glad to be away herself, in the deep sky, leaving the Atlantic behind and heading toward the Pacific. I sensed too that she was resigned, turned fatalistic. She had no choice but to take her chances with her new owner. With a tank of gas she was ready to fly for five hours straight if he wanted, 75 miles per hour.

If he wants to crash me, he's going to crash me.

The engine instruments practiced harmony … all at the temperatures and pressures they ought be, all steady as though the indicator needles had been painted on their dials. It takes a while, flying a new airplane, to discover just what Normal is for each instrument, and when they're all steady on one's first cross-country flight, that's a good start to a relationship, mechanical or human.

In less than an hour I eased the throttle back and began the descent for landing on the lake by my house. Once more the checklist as I had memorized it: "This is a WATER landing: left wheel's UP, tailwheel's UP, right wheel's UP, wheels indicate UP for a WATER landing; flaps are twenty degrees, boost pump is ON. This is a WATER landing and the wheels are UP!"

By now it's second nature, nose down to hold 75 mph, turn … now, slicing down through warm air. Double check out loud, "The wheels are UP for a WATER landing." Now the lake's beginning its ground-rush, feels like falling toward a sea of maple syrup. Break the rush with back pressure on

the control stick, ease the nose up as the airspeed slows, inches above the dark waves … hold it here, Richard, don't do nothin' but hold this perfect picture, and flik-flik-flik as the keel brushes the tops of the waves, … sshhhhhh as the lift goes out of the wings, the 'Rey relaxing into water as she becomes a speedboat slowing to 30 mph through the wet.

A touch of throttle to keep her in speedboat mode, a sweeping wide turn now toward the beach, clean spray flying to the left as we turn to the right. The intensity of delight, of balancing that power and control in my hands, carving this lovely clean turn that no one will see but me and which I shall never forget … that's why Toad came this way, that's why I'm here.

In the dream world of space-time, a lovely flying-boat running high-speed, skiing this level liquid snow—for some of us there's nothing to match. For all a pilot's discipline, for all the memorizing speeds and engine limits and procedures, for all the talking procedures aloud on one's drive to the grocery store, this moment's our payoff and we call it freedom.

Power easing off as we close on the beach, my airplane grateful that if her new owner can't remember takeoffs at least he hadn't forgotten landings, she slowed in the water while I push the control stick forward to keep the tail section from a wave-bashing. Now we're a family play-boat, idling toward the shore, water so close to the open hatch that I dangle my hand in cool wavelets. Flaps UP, boost pump OFF, radios OFF, headset off, seat belt released, wheels DOWN! Electric motors hum and press the landing gear down and locked ... in a few seconds we'll need wheels beneath us again to

drive up on the beach. Here it comes, throttle forward in a little roar of power, water falling away, and up we go, wheels rolling on sand.

Swing round to face the lake once again, brakes on, let the engine idle as temperatures stabilize. Quick scene-flashes of the flight just finished, that grand breath-taking ground-rush, the long curving ski-boat turn, the little 'Rey riding on air and water and speed.

If I've learned one lesson in all my days, it's this: *You can have all the experience in the world. If you don't use it, you've got none at all. Never forget what you know.*

Then a brush of sweet sadness: ignition OFF, master switch OFF. One last brief shudder, the 'Rey mid-word:

Promise me pleas ...

No one was watching. If they were, they'd have seen a pilot unmoving, alone with his new airplane on that silent beach, two futures now locked together, stretching way out ahead where it's all just fog.

CHAPTER 6

On the Fourth Day, She Rested

Y ou likely grew up with the fable of the sun and the wind. "You are too gentle," said the Wind. "Let us have a test of our powers, and I shall prevail!"

"Very well," replied the Sun. "Here is our test. Which of us can quickest make yon traveller remove his coat?"

The Wind laughed for a task so simple, and began to blow upon the traveller and his tattered garment. As his frail jacket whipped and thrashed, the traveller caught it, and the more fiercely blew the Wind the more tightly the traveller did fasten upon his coat, so that it could not be moved.

The Wind at last whistled to stop, exhausted, and so began the gentle Sun to turn its face upon the traveller ...

That's the way it worked for me today. The wind was blowing hard, and nothing could make me fly.

It's a little difficult to see, but you might notice the cherry-lemon wind streamers tied beneath the SeaRey's wing. In calm air the streamers hang straight down; when the wind is gusting to 20 mph the streamers are flying though the SeaRey isn't. What to do?

On my one shoulder, an angel: "At this stage of your training, Richard, it is not wise for you to fly in a breeze much over ten miles per hour. You can

fly in stronger winds later, after you've gained experience and skill through patient practice, working step by step. You're not skilled enough to fly safely in this breeze."

From my other shoulder: "Piece of cake, old top! You're anxious to go flying, the sky's as blue as it gets, carpe diem, faint heart ne'er won fair lady, no guts no glory, angels fear to tread because they can't fly as well as you can after all you're the red-hot fighter pilot, remember?"

Had I not some years ago joined Club Captain Chicken, I might well have gone for the devil's chatter. Between my vows when I entered the company of those elite pilots and my unbelievably bad takeoff yesterday, I chose the path of righteousness.

Soon as I made that Right Decision, a sound in the sky, a faint thunder growing louder:

Enter stage right the one and only Kermit Weeks, aloft in his 1926 Sikorsky S-39, practicing his first water landings in the old thing right amid my dreaded winds!

Travels with _Puff_

His timing, it was perfect to make me feel Wimpy the Fool. I turned to my angel shoulder, and she nodded bravely. "The Sikorsky is nine times heavier than the SeaRey, my dear. A sea too rough for you in the 'Rey is not too rough for Kermit's big flying boat!"

I sighed. "He's going to say I'm a sponge."

"He may say this. When he does, ask him how many guardian angels he's gone through, how many have quit his shoulder in disgust. Do you know about his takeoff in the Quicksilver with the leaking floats, when all the water rushed to the back as soon as he took off, left him hanging ten feet in the air, at zero airspeed? Did he mention his low-level slow-roll in the Spitfire when the bolt fell loose and locked his ailerons? Did he bother to share with you the time…"

"Can you at least have his engine get drowned in the spray, Angel, so he has to drift helpless till some boat comes and rescues him?"

"Richard," my angel murmured, "we do not wish ill on others lest it return to plague ourselves."

I spent the rest of my day sitting on the bed splicing line for a rudder lock. After that was finished I found some Shredded Wheat things to put in a bowl with milk for dinner. Next I thought I might write to say how virtue feels, acting on one's angel judgment instead of going all foolish and maybe breaking one's new airplane in a rogue wind-gust to 40, which is what I am doing.

If I've learned one lesson in all my days, it's this: *Live to our highest right and we feel an easy-rolling lift of spirit. Sell ourselves for less and our skateboard's gone iron cobblestones.*

There is not a scratch on my little SeaRey this evening, and that is because when it's her life at stake I most often listen to reason. Let my fine judgment be an example to other red-hot fighter pilots when they choose to assay the independence of seaplane flying, centuries hence.

I trust it shall be so, because right now it's frustrating as doom to sit on the ground and listen to the wind. And we haven't even started flying home.

CHAPTER 7

Ev-ry-one Knows It's Win-dy

When you need to get an airplane pilot's attention, say, "Gusts to ...," and add a number like forty. When you get that look of immediate concern, then you can change the subject and talk about anything you want. Doesn't need any context. Just the phrase, and watch what happens.

So did the weather folks get my attention along with everyone else's first thing this morning when they forecast gusts to 25 for this afternoon. Since I am a new pilot to the SeaRey, they don't have to say "... forty-two ..." to make me look like a deer in headlight season. When they say "twenty-five," they mean the speed in knots, or nautical miles per hour, so of course you multiply that number by 1.15 to convert to Look out, that's 30 miles per hour!

I'm wide awake, thinking:

If they're right about the winds, I won't be able to fly, even that short way north to the SeaRey factory, meet Dan Nickens and fly with Kerry Richter, though I promised to be there. I'll be trapped in the Winter Haven Wind Bubble for who knows how long. Since the wind is only ten miles per hour right this minute, why don't I simply take off and meet them now, instead of waiting till tomorrow?

No sooner done than said, and here I was on the beach removing cockpit and engine covers, inspecting the airplane for its flight, stuffing all I want to take with me aboard the SeaRey.

Forty minutes later I'm looking down at Tavares, Florida, America's Seaplane City, the lovely lake-town which decided to welcome flying boats to city center! Shortly after it decided, Tavares hosted seaplane fly-ins, tourists came to watch, the economy picked up. Other towns with waterfront don't much care for seaplanes, so which one are you gonna fly to on a bright weekend?

Tavares was, in fact, in the midst of a Splash-In for seaplanes, but by the time I arrived, the wind had picked up a bit more, and two dozen other planes were all arrived and tied down on the shore. The 'Rey and I circled overhead.

"What do you think, ma'am?" (I don't have a name for my airplane.)

Windy.

"M," I replied.

There were long white wind-streaks on the water, whitecaps on Lake Dora. It was comfy for the two of us, a thousand feet overhead, but the water down there was short and choppy.

Quartering tailwind to the seaplane ramp.

"M-hm. Not so hot."

And the ramp's not very wide.

"No," I replied, "it isn't."

Richard, to be honest with you, I'm scared. I can see me bashing my wing on ... do you see those steel bars by the ramp? Unless we make a perfect approach in all this wind, I'm going to get hurt.

"You don't trust me, ma'am, to make a perfect approach?"

Silence.

"Well, then," I said. "Let's try somewhere else, and if everything's bad we'll go land at an airport."

Thank you.

She was happy I remembered—because she's an amphibian, we have choices.

We flew south a mile or two and there was the SeaRey factory, with its smaller lake, not yet so wind-whipped. There the buildings, turning below, where she had been manufactured, her parts crated in an assembly kit shipped to her first owner.

"Home Sweet Home?" I asked.

I don't remember. It's hazy. I was just parts.

"What do you think? Let's land?"

There's no beach, Richard.

"See the ramp?"

It's a narrow ramp. It's high, too. If I fall off ...

"I think we can do it."

Silence for a while as we circled overhead. Then, sudden resolve:

I think we can do it, too.

It made me happy, to hear her say that.

I eased the throttle back. "This will be a WATER landing," I said. I looked at the landing gear. "Left wheel's UP; tailwheel's UP; right wheel's UP; wheels indicate UP for a WATER landing." I touched the flap control switch for three and a half seconds, checked the flaps motoring down as we slowed, switched the fuel boost pump ON. "Flaps are down, boost pump's on, wheels are UP for a WATER landing."

The propeller whispering behind us, I held the nose down, watching the lake as it turned and began its rush up toward us. "Snuggle down to the water, Richard," I told myself aloud, "Nose up just a bit ..." It was me or a little gust of wind, the 'Rey settled quicker than I hoped, touched the water, bounced a few inches into the air, touched again, skated smoothly over the wavetops then settled into her slow-boat mode, purring softly through the water.

I pressed right rudder to turn, but the wind was strong enough that little seaplane couldn't complete the attempt before she stopped, swung her nose left, weathervaning. I let it swing left, then added left rudder, using the momentum of the turn and a little burst of power to carry us round. That worked, and we taxied downwind toward the ramp.

I pressed the microphone button. "Anybody home at SeaRey?"

In a minute, "... SeaRey just landed?"

I was glad to hear a voice, even part of a sentence. "SeaRey Three Four Six Papa Echo. We'd like to try the ramp, if that's OK."

"It's a little narrow," came the radio, "and you're going to want a good amount of power to come up." A figure appeared near the head of the ramp, with a handheld radio. It was Kerry Richter, president of Progressive Aerodyne, the SeaRey company. He wasn't expecting me, I remembered, till tomorrow. He was wondering who this strange newcomer could be, and hoping whoever we were, we could handle the ramp.

"You want to make a long straight approach, with this wind, keep it straight, and when you're close to the ramp you want to give her plenty of power to come up."

"Roj." (Which is short for "Roger," which is short for "I understand." … but I do not care to take a lot of time talking about this because I am setting up my approach to the ramp and my airplane is frightened that I'll miss it in this wind and she'll fall off that six-foot drop, and it will hurt.)

I lowered the wheels, managed to find the right power setting and rudder to keep her cruising straight toward the ramp. If I lost control and she weathervaned here, it would not be fun.

The steel of the ramp angled up out of the water a hundred feet ahead … seventy feet ahead. I brought the throttle forward and the 'Rey picked up speed. Wheels touched metal underwater and I pressed more power, the engine roaring out, water cascading from the wheels and hull as we lifted from the wet, she changing to a land creature before our eyes. I couldn't see the right side of the ramp, but hoped if I kept the left wheel a couple feet from the left edge of the thing, the right wheel would take care of itself.

The 'Rey said nothing, not breathing, eyes closed, while we roared up that incline.

Then all at once we were whisking down the ramp to a level parking area: throttle back, engine ticking over at idle under the windy sun, as though we did this every day.

She let out a long breath. *God love you, pilot.*

There alongside us was another SeaRey, inside the big hangar were a dozen more, aircraft in all stages of construction, some for assembly into kits, some ready to fly. I shut the engine down and the 'Rey went fast asleep.

It had been a year since I had flown with Kerry, back when this moment was barely a hope in my unknown future.

"Hi Richard. That's a beautiful airplane you have!" He looked for detail, moved the seat back aside, noticed construction. "Nice," he said. "Jim Ratte does good work. You've got a fine airplane."

That was pleasant to hear. I called Dan Nickens, to say I'd arrived a little early. I hadn't met Dan in person, but he'd helped me the year before, took hours from his days answering my questions about SeaReys. It was Dan who had flown to Valkaria on my behalf and inspected this airplane before I arrived. He reported she had been well built and worth more than her asking price. At last we'd meet Dan.

He appeared a few minutes later, a tall calm gentleman, the easy way about him of a favorite high-school teacher.

"You did it!" he said, turning to the airplane, touching her wing. "You'll love her. I guess you already do."

"You guess right, Dan."

The day dissolved into lunch and talk, and here am I this evening in a quiet antique hotel in Mount Dora, looking toward an early start tomorrow, flying with Kerry and Dan for my advanced SeaRey training sessions.

If I've learned one lesson in all my days, it's this: *If we want adventure in our lives, nobody's going to make it happen but us.*

CHAPTER 8

Is There Such a Thing as Bad News?

I've got good news, and I've got bad news, and I've got good news again, so don't let the second phrase frighten you the way it did me. Everything's OK now, after a day of high-level training with Dan, me on a near-vertical learning curve.

For about the hundredth time I've heard and now I hear myself saying it, too: one does need special instruction in the SeaRey to fly it safely and well. It is not complicated training, but no matter you're an airline captain no matter how sweet be this little lady, you just plain need air-time with her to learn habits that will keep you happy in the long run.

Oh dear, where do I start? This morning. Got a little plastic bottle of orange juice on the way to the SeaRey factory, was so needful of breakfast that I drank most all of it by the time I got to the cash register. The cashier said, "That will be $1.59." I told her, "But it's only half full!" She smiled and accepted my two dollars.

When we pulled the SeaRey out, Dan settled into the right seat (the place for co-pilots and instructors), and in the quiet before engine start, he said, "I want to say something before we fly."

"Yes, sir," I said, wondering why so solemn.

"I want you to understand that I know this is your airplane. I will not touch the controls unless you specifically ask me to do so."

Never have I heard this from a flight instructor, and never had I said such a thing when I was instructing. You want instant indicator of character? With courtesy like that you know this is going to be a good hour together.

"Why, Dan," I said, "if I somehow throw us into an outside inverted flat spin, I'd appreciate it if you would take the controls. Or if I get into any trouble, you say, 'I've got the airplane,' and fly us out of it."

He nodded, unsmiling. I was to discover that Dan has a wide, subtle sense of humor, but on this subject there was no kidding. "I understand I have your permission to do that if it is necessary," he said. I wondered what the story might be that made this preflight statement important for him to say, but I didn't ask.

Engine started and warmed, we taxied down the ramp, slowly, slowly … the SeaRey a dancer easing down a tightrope to her stage.

Dan asked me to do the engine run-up on the water. Unusual, I thought, when we could have done it on the land, yet it was more thoughtful of others nearby.

"This will be a WATER takeoff," I said. "Left wheel's UP, tailwheel's UP, right wheel's UP, wheels indicate UP, flaps are 20, boost pump's on, trim is set. Are you ready for takeoff, Dan?"

"Any time."

I eased the throttle forward. The little seaplane charged ahead, and swiftly we were airborne. I finished my after-takeoff check.

"I know you're being kind to the engine," said Dan, "but at those slower speeds—did you hear the water going through the propeller on takeoff?"

I shook my head. Wasn't paying attention.

"You want to keep the spray out of the prop as much as you can, so if you go ahead and push that throttle right on in, smoothly but faster, that'll make it easier on the propeller."

Of course, I thought. I remember best when I know the reasons for things.

In a few minutes we were over Lake Apopka, a huge round body of water, and shallow. Because of the shallow, while there were long white wind-streaks on the water, the waves weren't high. My first water landing went well. "You don't need to hold the stick back or forward when you're coming off the step," said Dan. "Just let it be where it wants to be, that'll be fine."

We floated serene on the water, engine purring softly. "This time I'd like to see you give it some quick back-pressure at around fifty miles per hour. Pop the stick back quickly and hold it. The airplane will hop up into ground effect and hang there, and you can pick up speed in the air. It gets you off the water a bit faster."

"Ground effect" is the term for the discovery that airplane wings are more efficient when they're flying closer than half their wingspan above the water. Dan explained that we could fly for miles in ground effect, fly faster and longer there, and I remembered that Jonathan Seagull had learned the same thing, early in his own training. How much of my life, I wondered, would follow his? Not much, came the answer.

I tried the hop-takeoff and it worked, and had me smiling. I had never done such a thing before.

"Now this time after we touch down on the water," he said, "I want you to let it slow to about thirty miles per hour, and then just stomp on the rudder and slide us sideways for a quick-stop. Keep the wings level, of course."

That sounded a bit aggressive to me, but next landing as we slowed he shouted, "Slide! Slide!"

I gritted my teeth and pushed hard on the left rudder pedal, holding the wings level with opposite aileron. The world spun sideways and slid, spray flying. We were stopped almost instantly, then moving gently ahead. "If you have to stop fast," he said. "Of course you don't want to do that in rough water."

We hopped up into the air again, this time for a lesson in beaching on a lake near the Tiki Bar restaurant. With plenty of power after we landed, the 'Rey walked out of the shallow water near the beach, turned back toward the water and stopped on dry sand.

I shut down the engine.

"Lunch?" Dan asked.

We had something to eat, watching the pretty sight of the airplane resting on the beach, no runways, no taxiways, no control tower … just herself, on the sand.

Another SeaRey circled overhead, sifted down to the water, taxied and parked not far away. "It's not unusual," said Dan. "You're parked on the

beach, another 'Rey sees you there and comes down to land." He smiled. "Of course this is a popular place for lunch, and they like us to come in. See?" he pointed. "They put up a wind sock for us."

After lunch we found a little airport with a soft grass runway to practice landings. The 'Rey was the perfect lady, no bounding all over the countryside, landings or takeoffs. After the third landing, Dan asked me to stop, let him out of the airplane, so I could get the feel of the airplane without his weight and to let him take photos of my landings.

The perfect lady. Three-point landings smooth and gentle, an easy rolling touch on the green field, as she changed from air-creature to land-creature.

A full stop landing to let Dan back aboard, then off again for the short flight to the SeaRey factory lake. On the way I looked for lift under the cumulus clouds, to help us climb. Dan felt the bump and whoosh of a thermal, lifting us. "Do you fly sailplanes?" he asked.

"I used to," I told him. "One doesn't forget."

He nodded. "You set the rpm around thirty-eight hundred, gives her the sink rate of a glider. Sometimes I'll fly all afternoon, use about no fuel."

So we chased thermals for a while, rising in their lift, the propeller whisking quietly behind us.

"Slow flight?" I asked.

"Fine."

I eased the stick back, slowed the 'Rey to 50, 45 ... 40 mph.

"Ever done a takeoff stall in this airplane?"

I shook my head no.

"You might ease the nose up and add full power. Tell me when the wing stalls."

I did as he asked, but the 'Rey didn't stall, didn't break and drop away from a too-steep climb as would other airplanes. Instead, she mushed along at 30-something mph, climbing two hundred feet per minute.

"To stall full power," he said, "you have to whip-stall her. If you're gentle, ease the nose up, she'll just hang there and climb all day long."

Every one of these events, these learning-jumps, got me liking the little plane all the more. She can do so much! For nearly two hours we continued our lesson, the hatch slid back. Water takeoffs with the hatch open, one gets a few cool drops of lake-water in one's hair, on one's shirt, cooling liquid fun.

We landed at last at the factory lake, a step turn to line on the ramp. Then slowed, wheels down and under water, the 'Rey lined on the ramp.

"Ramp's a little narrow," he said. "I can see the right wheel and you can't … would you like me to ramp it?"

Remembering yesterday's ramp adventure: "Please do, Dan. You have the airplane."

"I have the airplane," he said, and lowered the wheels.

We motored to the ramp and a strange thing happened … in shallow water, the wheels bounced on an underwater sandbar and one tire missed the edge of the ramp. The 'Rey shuddered to a stop.

"No worries," Dan said. "I'll get out here and push you back into the water. She'll do better without my weight aboard and you can bring her up."

He stepped out of the cockpit into the shallow water, the 'Rey floating higher than before. Dan pushed us backward, then we motored in a wide turn to set up for an approach to the ramp. As soon as we were alone, she woke up talking.

What are you doing? Her voice, trembling in my mind.

"We're setting up for the ramp, ma'am."

I don't … I'm not … it's so narrow …

"Not to worry," I told her. "We did this yesterday."

I have a bad feeling.

"We'll do just fine."

Can we go somewhere else? The beach?

"We're home! This is your factory!"

Please?

"Come along, young lady," I said. "Close your eyes, we'll be at the hangar in half a minute."

She was silent.

I lined on the ramp, easy with a light breeze behind us. Sixty feet from the base of the ramp I pushed the throttle ahead and the 'Rey powered up

the metal roadway. Careful to allow the right wheel plenty of room on the ramp we sailed up the incline, till the left wheel drove off the edge on the other side.

I heard a crunching shuddering crashing sound, the cockpit lurched and dropped, slammed to a stop.

I swept the engine off at once, master switch off to kill the electrics.

"Damn!" I couldn't believe what I had done. "Damn it, Richard, damn damn damn you what you've done to her!"

Engine off electrics off, the little seaplane was feeling nothing. She was just a machine body, fainted half on, half off the ramp.

Dan was at the airplane in an instant. "No worries," he said. "This is an easy fix. We just lift her up ..."

"Oh, Dan, I am so ..." Damn damn *damn* Richard you clumsy, you dumb, stupid ...

"Really Richard, I'm telling you, this is not a problem for a SeaRey! She is light! She'll be back on her feet in no time!"

Part of me realized that raging at myself for running off the ramp does no good at all. It wasn't helping Dan or me or most of all, my little 'Rey. She was anesthetized, sound asleep, tilted there unmoving. The other part of me was gently astonished ... why was Dan so unflustered by my crash, so unmoved with my wrecking the airplane? A thought whipped through my mind: There's no disaster that can't become a blessing ... I dismissed it at once, so hypnotized with the appearance of the wreck that had been my aircraft.

I climbed out of the cockpit as damaged as my 'Rey. More damaged than she, it turned out. But she was not a pretty sight.

At least, I thought, you drove her off the low part of the ramp, her wheel dropped only a foot down into the mud. God protects stupid dumb damn ... how could you have done this to her!

"It looks like we got the float, too," said Dan, not much disturbed.

Sure enough, the left float smashed against a dike of earth and mud, its strut twisted and broken.

Dan knew what I must be thinking, me from my world of big heavy expensive airplanes. If this were a conventional seaplane, I'd be looking at weeks of repair.

"Aren't you glad you have a SeaRey?"

"Dan, of course I'm glad, but don't you see ..."

"Richard, you watch. I know you think this is a big deal, you slipped off the ramp and you bent a strut. Listen: This is not a big deal!"

We found a long wooden plank, used it to lever the wheel back up to the ramp.

"I'm going to push the airplane back into the water, swing her around and take her up the ramp to the hangar. Do you mind if I do that?"

"Yes I mind, Dan. I want to bring her up the ramp myself."

My twisted emergency humor ... trying the ramp again was the last thing I wanted to do. Dan didn't see the smile. "Sure. Of course, Richard. Now when you come around ..."

"Dan I was joking! Of course I want you to bring her up!"

He laughed, I think it was in relief, and in a minute he had powered the 'Rey out of the water and she was getting the attention of the men who had designed her.

In minutes the strut was replaced.

Dan had a point to make. "Some people say it's coincidence," he said, "and others say there's a reason for everything."

(Had the crash not happened, we would not have inspected the tail-wheel. Had we not inspected the tailwheel, we would not have found a bolt that was ready to fail, after some of my early disasters of landings. Not dangerous, but it may have been inconvenient, had it failed in the middle of New Mexico.)

"By the way," Dan said as he tightened it down, "the list price of that strut that just broke is twenty-three dollars."

An aviator of any experience can estimate the cost of a repair by the sound it makes as breaks. The sound I heard was a $2,600 crunch. I need to recalibrate my hearing, I discovered, for the lightness and simplicity of my SeaRey.

Dan was right, of course, this was not a big deal at all. I took back quite a few damns I had said, while leaving most of the stupids.

I thought it might be, and sure enough, today was an interesting day. Around sunset, Dan turned to me. "I've been thinking about flying my 'Rey to Seattle," he said. "You'll be on your way pretty soon. Would you mind if I flew alongside?"

If I've learned one lesson in all my days, it's this: *There's no way to tell bad news from good as it's happening. We'll find out which the moment we realize, long-term, it's all good.*

CHAPTER 9

Learning Secrets

Kerry and I had agreed to meet at 9 am, so at 8:30 I stopped at the gas station mini-market for my breakfast drink. I thought it was a bottle of milk I was buying, but when I drank it tasted unmilklike and I noticed the word Vanilla where I might have expected *Milk* to have been. I didn't read any more, but made a note to provide this public service announcement that just because a bottle is white and it is surrounded by milk bottles don't take one and buy it without checking to be sure unless what you want is Vanilla.

Arrived early, I walked out the grass to the Devil's Ramp, the arena for the temporary grief and permanent blessing of yesterday. There were our footprints yet, deep in the mud, and I imagined them a hundred million years from now, turned to stone, proof there had been bipedal lifeforms on the planet millennia before the Rise of the Gerbil as the dominant life on Earth.

There was a whisper in the sky, and I looked up. It was Dan Nickens' SeaRey, and in the still of the morning I heard for the first time how quiet are these machines. His plane curved gently down from altitude, floating on air, settled soft and silent as thistledown on the ripples of the lake.

He taxied toward the Ramp from Hell, his airplane's innocent left wing sweeping toward the wall of earth left by the falling water level of the lake.

Sixty feet out, the engine powered up, white water at the 'Rey's bow, and up the Ramp of Death they came, Dan and his airplane. Sure enough, the left float brushed the top of the muddy wall, a black smear on the snowy surface.

I winced for the sight of it, though nothing bent or broke.

Kerry arrived as Dan shut the engine down and stepped from his machine.

It felt strange to say it, but someone had to speak. "Kerry? Dan? I'm a frog from a different hot-water pot, I can see what you must be missing because it's happening so slowly. The lake level's dropping, maybe it's just a quarter-inch per day. But when you of all pilots, Dan, are brushing your wing floats on the mud, coming up that ramp, that's wrong!"

Kerry nodded. "Got to do something about that. Maybe widen the ramp. But that'll take a couple of days …" said in the tone of a seaplane-company president who can ill afford to lose two days' access to the water.

Kerry slipped into the right seat of my airplane, I started the engine and we eased down La Rampa del Diablo; the seaplane's right float we couldn't help it brushing the mud.

Dan had gone before us, and both seaplanes taxied duck-like, circling on the water. Then we were off in twin clouds of flying spray, lifting over the fields southward. Kerry flew the plane as Dan shadowed us from above, floating up-sun taking pictures.

Then we were off to our training.

Orlando North is a concrete airstrip lying east-west on the ground. The wind was from the south, a perfect, direct crosswind. Yet such was my confidence that the 'Rey and I were at last becoming friends, that I was not much terrified at the sight of hard-surface crosswind landings. And as a man thinketh about runways, so shall it be, for we made landings both directions and the little machine was every bit the lady, touching gently and rolling straight, landing after landing.

Kerry had been ready for a scary time—what if it wasn't the tailwheel that had been askew, but the pilot? "Does she feel better to you now?" he asked.

I stopped smiling long enough to talk. "Way better!"

South we headed for water landing instruction. Kerry has a reputation amongst the SeaRey family of being the best pilot of them all … he has nearly as many hours flying this one aircraft as I've flown in some 140

different airplanes over half a century. Things that can kill you in other sea-planes he has engineered out of the 'Rey.

We touched down on the water, for instance, and while we still raced along, jet-ski-like on the step and before I could scream, he pushed the control stick all the way forward.

Instead of the nose plowing instantly underwater, windshield and canopies blasting away and us upside down kicking free of sudden wreckage, the nose bobbed down, and up, and down again, and up as she raced along. Control stick to neutral and the bobbing stopped. My instructor explained why that was so, something about hydrodynamics of the C-model hull, but I don't do well remembering technical data while recovering from a near-death experience.

We spent ten minutes racing along on the step, streaking the surface of the big lake, spray a slalom-trail behind us. He talked me through tight step-turns.

"If you lower the nose, now, in your turn, and come up with the power … go ahead and come up with the power … see how much tighter you can turn with the keel in the water? Now bring the nose up a bit … and the turn shallows out."

Once I would not dared to have pushed that stick forward an inch, now I was doing it slowly, carefully watching the turn rate change as I did. It was a grand demonstration of the way the little machine can turn at high speed.

After an hour on the water we flew home, chatting about the habits of the airplane, circled to land on the short axis of the small lake at the factory. At first it felt strange, watching the opposite shore so close and closing fast,

Learning Secrets

but I had learned not to let appearances frighten me, knowing the 'Rey could land with room to spare. I leveled at the surface, she touched gently down, slowed to a walk on the water.

I was not eager to face the Ramp of Despair, so Kerry guided us into the weeds at the water's edge near the factory, unfastened his shoulder harness and stepped ashore.

"Thank you Kerry!" Knowing he couldn't understand how deeply I meant those words.

He smiled and waved. No big deal.

How many times has he done this, I thought, one more fledgling sent quacking into the sky, old fears sunk to the bottom of the sea?

The 'Rey sang along the surface of the lake, vaulted happy into the air. We half-circled to fly over the factory, and my last view of Kerry Richter was his wave, half a thousand feet below. Soon he was lost to sight, and the factory, disappeared over the horizon behind us. How many lives, I wondered, how many human lives had that one man changed with his ideas and engineering and designs?

We have lives, too, don't forget. Except for him, I wouldn't be in the air.

She startled, her words in my mind. So much dual flying I've done, lately, taking my training, and she speaks only when we fly alone. Alone, one cannot help feeling close to one's aircraft. We need each other, to fly, and from that need an intimacy is born between flesh and metal.

"Excuse me, ma'am," I said. "I don't mean to be too friendly too soon, but I have this feeling that you and I, we'll be ... I don't even know what to call ..."

Do I need a name, Richard?

I smiled. "Do I, ma'am?"

A young, amused silence.

Puff. Call me Puff. I'm the cloud that's almost here, almost gone. I'm the wistful melody, known but half-remembered, calling you higher. I'm the wisp in the air no one sees but you, dear pilot. I'm the life no one else believes is true.

I said it quietly, midst the gentle thunder of wind over her open cockpit: "Hi, Puff."

If I've learned one lesson in all my days, it's this: *You want a bright and lovely time on earth? Set your imagination free, and trust it to lift you over mountains!*

CHAPTER 10

Rough Water, Triple Ties and Storms Which May Never Be

This morning, schedule-free, I was out to say hi to Puff just after sunrise. I spent hours messing about with her, making a simple parking brake, a seat belt mod so I don't have to fumble so much for the buckle, buying bits and pieces at the hardware store for her tool-kit, a label-maker to renew her placards, batteries for the noise-cancelling headsets, a light bungee for aileron trim assist ... bits and pieces by way of customizing her to me, and me to her.

It was calm all morning, the wind picking up in the afternoon, when I needed to go flying. Just after two pm we rolled off the beach into the lake, I felt the support shift from wheels to the hull and Puff became a boat.

Wheels retracted as the engine warmed, we taxied to the downwind end of the lake, the end where the waves begin kicking up a bit. She taxied happily crosswind, tips of the waves sometimes splashing a few drops into the cockpit. I've been finding it hard to close the hatch, it's such pleasure to fly with the top down, feeling the wind.

Today we were light on fuel, eight gallons aboard, nearly two hours' flying though I prefer to land for the day with an hour's reserve. Rarely do I use that reserve, it's a peace-of-mind issue with me, and with most other pilots, too.

(Just now I realized that I'm turning you into an aviation buff: " … light on fuel, gusts to forty, the four most useless things to a pilot: altitude above you, runway behind you, fuel in the gas truck and a tenth of a second ago." It may not be what you signed up for with this book, but it comes at no extra charge.)

Throttle forward (swiftly forward, Dan … I've not dawdled on the throttle for water takeoffs since you mentioned it puts water through the propeller), and in nine seconds Puff was flying.

She was a bit alarmed, a few minutes later, looking down at the wind-streaks on the lake I had picked for practice.

You're not going to land, are you?

"Of course we're going to land, Puff, we need the rough-water practice."

Do you want me to go to sleep?

I think airplanes call that "wry humor," her way of asking whether I think we may be crashing soon.

"It's a normal procedure, Puff. Rough-water landings, remember?"

No.

I said my checklist. "This will be a WATER landing. Left wheel's UP, tailwheel's UP, right wheel's UP, wheels indicate UP for a WATER landing, boost pump's on flaps 20."

She was not complaining, just feeling cautious about my flying skills after our crash on the Ramp of Despair. Power back, we slid down final approach. The water blue-violet, an occasional warning-flag whitecap here and there in the wind.

I set for a normal landing, and before we touched the first wave, Puff knew I was screwing it up. She didn't say anything, but I felt her stiffen for the impact, water at 55 mph having about the pillowness of concrete. We struck the first wave, bounced, bounced again, bounced higher and I came in with power to fly away and try again.

That's our rough-water landing? That's how we do it, just like a normal landing except we bounce instead of stay down?

"I'm sorry, Puff. I didn't think it was that rough. NOW we will do our true rough-water landing."

Next try: "This will be a WATER landing, left wheel's UP …"

Is this what life is going to be like for us? Are we always going to be pushing boundaries, we'll be doing this forever, you and me?

She asked, so far as I could tell, with no agenda, no hope for me to be someone different. She was curious to know what the future might be holding for us and felt she was entitled to ask. I think she was puzzled when I smiled, since she didn't mean to be funny.

"I don't think of this as 'pushing boundaries,' Puff." We turned onto final approach into the wind, this time me remembering the difference between a normal and a rough-water landing. Hold her off, stall her into the water, dead slow, so there will be no bouncing.

And sure enough, at the slower speed the water was softer, Puff splashed down and stayed down. Flying into the wind, we couldn't have been moving more than 30 mph when we touched the waves.

Better. You do have good flying skills ...

"Thank you, Puff."

... you just don't always use them.

She doesn't lie, this airplane.

I pushed the throttle forward and in a few seconds we were airborne again.

We did five or six more landings, till they were easy, and I knew we could handle rougher weathers than the lake had to offer that day.

We climbed at full power, and I brought her nose way up into the no-stall-but-pitching-climb mode almost unique to the SeaRey.

The dial on the left, the airspeed indicator, says we're flying at 16 mph. We may not really have been flying at 16 mph, because of instrument error at such a high angle of climb. But not many aircraft, even with airspeed errors, can show that speed while they're flying.

Then we leveled and turned for home, sped along by the wind. I had been flying with the top down, open cockpit on this warm day, and enjoyed the coolth where water-drops had splashed my shirt.

The lake at home wasn't so rough. We dropped down over Kermit's Fantasy of Flight, looking carefully for the barnstorming biplane there and found it on the ground, loading passengers.

"This is a WATER landing …" I said. Normal landing on the wavelets, touching softly, then power up to blaze speedboatlike toward the beach.

As we approached the shore, we slowed and I put the wheels down to taxi up onto the sand.

I'm getting used to you. Thank you for keeping me off the ramp, yesterday. I know you were scared of it, too, after what happened.

"Oh, I wouldn't say 'scared.'"

I would.

The shore loomed closer.

We're going to get along, aren't we?

"Wheels are down for the beach," I said, and smiled. "We're going to get along just fine, Puff."

Wheels touched sand underwater, I pushed the throttle forward and she rose like Venus from the sea, going taller than she is on the water. She turned and stopped on her marks, and in a minute I shut the engine down. What a magnificent airplane, I thought in the quiet.

Thunderstorms tonight, said the computer, could be storms tonight.

My response was to triple-tie Puff's wings and tail to anchors in the ground, pull on the cockpit cover and wrap a tarp around the engine. She'll be fine, I thought. Except for big hail, which probably, like the storms themselves, won't be happening.

If I've learned one lesson in all my days, it's this: *There are powers which can wreck the stage-sets in our world of appearances. There's no power can kill the forever-spirit of who we are.*

CHAPTER 11

A Different Family

*I*t's been one year, from the day of my first demonstration flight in a SeaRey, and this year, materialized by the power of thought, it was Puff and me together at the SeaRey Splash-In.

After all our preparation for the winds and storms, the weather split in two, storms passing to north and south, leaving just a few raindrops overnight for us. Just as well, thought I, happier to prepare for a storm and have it not arrive than prepare for it and have it smash us flat.

We watched the back of the weather slide eastward at dawn, and counted ourselves prepared to share blue sky and blue water and introduce ourselves to a dozen other 'Reys.

Turned out there were not a dozen, but 18 SeaReys at the picnic. Puff getting her share of kind words: "What a pretty airplane!" "Is this a Jim Ratte aircraft? He does fine work, doesn't he?"

Later we flew, and had this photo been snapped two minutes earlier, you would have seen perfect cloud-letters spelling her name. You can still see shards left, of the letters: P U F F.

Then this photo caught Puff and her shadow, our future: 3,300 miles flying low-level across a continent:

Patience, fortitude, believing. If I've learned one lesson in all my days, it's this: *All things come to those who know that what we hold in thought is what we shall see in our pretend lifetimes on our cardboard planets.*

CHAPTER 12

A Tour for Puff

Dan called at 10:30 this morning, while I was pre-flighting Puff, checking her cables and fastenings, engine and propeller to make sure she was ready to fly.

"It's going to the airshow or flying, and if you say flying, I'm ready to go." What a fine invitation, so you know what I replied.

"I'd like to show you the south St. Johns River," he said. "I'm getting fueled, I'll meet you in the air, an hour from now."

Like clockwork. I dropped into formation with him and we headed east, for Puff's first lesson in river flying, and mine. I sensed that what Dan had in mind was not so much showing me the river, but that he needed to know that Puff and I were ready for a major crosscountry flight.

I wonder how many hours Dan and his airplane 220WT (Whisky Tango, in pilot talk) have flown at altitudes less than a hundred feet. At less than ten feet. Puff got her first hour down there today. This is a whole new life for her, flying without quite so much crashing, and her little heart was happy and beating fast.

"I'm getting hungry," said Dan over the radio, hours and miles behind us. "Stop for lunch?"

"That's affirmative," I said. Pilots can't just say, "Yes." as that could be distorted on a poor radio to sound like "No," or "I'm not really sure." "That's affirmative," sounds like Yes.

I watched from above as he circled and landed on the river, not far from a restaurant which sells dinner and airboat rides. It was my first serious full-stop and leave the airplane for a while river landing. The wind was gentle, water smooth. Puff was not so sure about being left while we had lunch, but Dan has done this a thousand times.

"People are respectful and keep their distance from the planes," he said. Then he amended that. "You do have to be careful of nine-year-old boys. They like touching the controls and switches."

LOOK OUT!

Just kidding. While we spotted all sorts of alligators as we flew, none were harmed to make this photo:

Lunch, and we were off again, another river landing, not a soul in sight:

Hours of flying together build trust. Puff and 220WT, whose real name is Jennifer, are becoming good friends.

Tomorrow is the big Splash-In on the lake at Fantasy of Flight. Puff will be there in her colors, I will be, too.

The Puffster and I both went where we've never been before today, and we're learning fast.

If I've learned one lesson in all my days, it's this: *Don't worry what we're supposed to learn this time around. Follow what we most love in all the world, and we'll learn it.*

Thank you Dan from Puff and me for the tour and the flying instruction! Four hours' flying, not only at no charge, but the instructor bought lunch!

CHAPTER 13

A Tour for Puff, Part II

She didn't much care for me calling her "the Puffster," she feels it is harsh and coarse and casual and flip and chummy, it lacks respect and character and class and don't I care for her spirit after all don't I even want to be the least bit kind or thoughtful? I couldn't sleep last night because of it and now I have publicly to apologize: I am sorry Puff I shall never use that name again.

I am slow, learning how properly to address her … most aircraft are "she," but never have I flown so feminine an airplane.

Follows here a gallery of photos from the flight yesterday. Dan has flown the Florida back country in his SeaRey for years, now, but he was having as much fun as Puff and me.

Dan's looking back from Jennifer, this view of Puff off for the first time to see a world she's never known.

Little Puff,
big wilderness

Way
wilderness!

Lonely Lookin'
Sand

Dan and Jennifer landed on the water (not far from the alligator), Puff not quite ready to join them

Later, on an
elegant river,
she came down

After the wilderness, it felt a little strange, to be back in civilization.

Departing for home

Puff likes this picture, and is considering that she may select Dan to be her designated photographer.

CHAPTER 14

Tomorrow Today

W hat to say about this flying?

I know: "!!"

The impression one gets of Dan Nickens, talking with him for a while, is that he is a thoughtful gentle man, of vast knowledge in a number of subjects: geology, chemistry and law for three that I know, and SeaReys for another. The kind of soul that one is happy to meet at the Club, surrounded by books in leather bindings, paintings of philosophers on silent walls. Think "gentle-man," and you have a beginning description of this person.

I met him this morning in the air, his SeaRey Jennifer a tiny dot above the horizon north. Puff and I climbed from the south watching the dot grow wings. "Whiskey Tango has you in sight," said Dan on the radio.

"Papa Echo, roger."

I counted to three, timing our turn to intercept, and Puff and I dropped into position near Jennifer's left wing, a hundred feet or so away. Remember "gentle-man."

In twenty miles we were over Florida wilderness, Jennifer put her nose down toward one of the xillion deserted lakes in central Florida, and Puff followed, faithful wing-lady she.

Dan leveled out between six and twenty-four inches above the wavelets, a comfortable cruising altitude for him. It is a breathtaking sight, his seaplane skimming the water, sunlight flashing on the water and on the curved glass of his windscreen.

Flying twice the speed of sound at 40,000 feet is swimming in glue, compared to 75 mph some eight inches above the wavetops. Trailing him was a dark streak on the water, mark of the downwash of air from his wings. From time to time, Dan eased Jennifer down so her keel teased a line of ice-color spray from the water. This was precision flying measured in inches, and Puff had to admit, from her own conservative altitude of three feet, that it was lovely to behold.

For a landplane to fly so low over the water would have been foolish and dangerous ... where do you land when the engine stops? In the water! But in a seaplane at that height, where do you land when the engine stops? In the water! (Seaplane pilots have a little joke. They say that any airplane can land in the water, but seaplanes can do it more than once.)

Then a shore appeared ahead and they swept gracefully up, Jennifer/Dan, several hundred feet, and began following the canal that is the Kissimmee River, straight as a tightrope through a tranquil sea of wild palmettos and emerald pasture.

Appeared a runway alongside the canal! White sand against the grasses, it was wide enough for an automobile ... in fact it was probably used by automobiles. But Jennifer took it for a runway, her wheels swung down and I heard Dan's voice on the radio, "Wheels are down, for a land landing." Puff and I turned and watched from the air as they glided downward, touching softly, in a quick trail of white dust and sand, rolling true along the centerline then turning onto the grass alongside, swinging round to watch our landing.

I don't think ... I don't think I've ever done this.

When I didn't respond, except for, "This is a LAND landing. Left main is DOWN, tailwheel is DOWN, right main is DOWN, wheels are DOWN, indicate DOWN for a LAND landing,"

... on a road.

"It isn't a road, Puff. It's a narrow runway."

Oh! All right, then.

And we landed on the road. When we pulled off onto the grass, I said, "I've never done that before ..."

WHAT?

"I've landed in hayfields, pastures, beaches. Never on a road."

In your LIFE?

"In my life."

She was quiet for a minute.

It's just a narrow runway …

I was still smiling when I shut her engine down.

Remember Dan is a refined gentleman, refined, studious, reads books? Now he's landing on abandoned roads, and you haven't heard the rest of the day. Can gentle men be so skilled, flying airplanes, that what sets the heart racing for us is for them a different aspect of refinement? Or does their heart race, too, back at the Club, thinking on this day?

Perhaps he needs to know, before he launches cross-country with Puff and her pilot … do these two know how to fly?

I'll let his photos give their answers, but I must comment on the Reed Encounter. The field of reeds is on the west side of Lake Okeechobee, and the tops of the reeds stand six feet plus above the water. Dan was flying at his usual altitude but I noticed Jennifer was not climbing to clear the reeds. I heard, "Wheels up for a water landing," Jennifer slowed, then all at once disappeared in a forest of green.

Richard, we're not …?

"If they can do it, we can do it," I told her. "He's showing us what he's learned."

What they've learned.

"Wheels are up for a water landing," I said, and touched the flap switch to DOWN. We hit the reeds at 50 miles per hour, in a cloud of spray and a rippling hush of willowy stems bending away before us. When we slowed, still pushing reeds aside, I caught a glimpse of Jennifer's vertical stabilizer as she swung toward shore, into a deep section of

green. Now just the tip of her propeller was visible above the sea of foliage, Dan maneuvering to get a photo of Puff in Reeds.

He got it.

A gentle-man does not allow his skills to diminish, nor does he avoid adventure. For next up was the Bicycle Path.

From the air after we left the land of reeds, we saw a fine-tip pencil line through the marshes of southern Florida, an airboat roadway. Ten feet wide, straight as a die for a mile through the swamps. Shallow water, solid ground on each side.

When I heard, "Wheels up for a water landing," I thought what water? I screamed, silently, when I saw what Dan was planning.

He was planning to set Jennifer's hull on the airboat path, and let the wingtip floats clear the grass on each side by inches. But of course I knew the floats would be clearing the grass, by roughly an inch and a half. Only later did I find that Dan not only planned to make the landing, but to take photos as he did.

"There is no way that we're …" I said.

Piece of cake. If Jennifer can do it, I can do it.

"I guess you know what you're doing, Puff," I muttered. "Wheels are UP for a water landing." Where is she getting her confidence?

She was silent as we hushed down toward the slim trail of water. So far as I could tell, there was zero room for error. Ahead of us, Jennifer's bright wings stark against the wild grass, she touched the narrow stripe of water, spray flying white over the green on each side behind her.

"Boost pump's on, flaps are down, wheels are UP."

Then silence, two souls focused on what needed to be done. Just land her hull down that centerline, I thought, and her wings will take care of themselves. If Jennifer can do it …

Then the horizon turned green, a single slash of silver water ahead. Nail that silver, Puff, nail it down!

Which she did, her wake of liquid snow blowing into the air around us. Keep it straight at fifty miles per hour, nothing matters but keep it straight. Which we managed to do. I will admit if Puff will not that after half a minute of this I was delighted to push the throttle forward and follow Dan and Jennifer back into the sky.

(Photo by Dan Nickens holding his camera in one hand, flying his airplane with the other. The only hint this is difficult is that he was too busy, at that moment, to level the camera.)

They say that flying is hours and hours of boredom, punctuated by moments of stark terror. Way overstated. Flying, at least with Dan and Jennifer that day, was hours of alert anticipation, punctuated by moments of let us say intense concentration.

Today, then, was four hours of alert intensity, watching a master of his aircraft, at play.

I know what Dan will say: "Don't go calling me any great pilot. I have a lot to learn!" So I won't call him any great pilot. Nice picture, Dan!

At the end of the day, Jennifer turned north toward home, Puff and I drifted down to land on home water, taxied up on our beach.

They're good, aren't they?

I was reaching for an understatement to reply.

Will we ever be that good in the air, you and me?

"If we train as hard as they do, fly as much as they do," I told her. "One day, Puff, yes. One day we will be that good in the air."

If I've learned one lesson in all my days, it's this: *It's the most difficult tests we face, when we pass 'em, make us happiest.*

CHAPTER 15

Otra Vez,
el Capitan Pollo

I cannot imagine what it must have been for Commander Richard Byrd, setting off on his expedition to the Antarctic in 1926. He had a big airplane to prepare for his flight.

How can such a little airplane need so many things to be ready for her trip? Puff has sent me shopping for a grease gun, KeelGuard, five different kinds of tape, Velcro, weatherstripping, power supply expander, corrosion-proofing spray, epoxy weld, sandpaper, gas cans, bolts, soft fabric, three kinds of rope, anchor and clevis and carabiners, small padlock, bungee cord, safety wire, tiedown stakes, a cockpit cover, an engine cover, light line for the rudder lock, spray wax (to polish her windscreen), tools, batteries, survival foods, bottled water and that's just to start.

I spent most of the day attaching the KeelGuard (lying under the plane, my body gradually disappearing in the sand), and making little things out of tape and Velcro.

But this is a story about Captain Chicken. Again.

Sometimes the wind blows during the day over Florida, then settles down in the afternoon. Sometimes it's gentle in the day and picks up toward afternoon. It depends, apparently, on whether I work on Puff in the morning or later on. Today the water looked flyable, a little breeze but not much, so I didn't bother to check the weather report. (Do you sense something unexpected about to happen?)

I got Puff ready to fly: tiedowns, cockpit and engine covers off, rudder lock off, preflight inspection complete. It didn't occur to me that I was on the up-wind side of the lake, so what I was seeing was the calm water. (That's the way unhappy things happen in aviation; chains of little events link themselves together to become, somewhere down the road, a big deal.)

Why do I call, "Prop clear!" before engine start when there's never anyone within a mile of the propeller? Habit, I guess. Then her engine fired and Puff was awake, a minute later rolling down the sand into the water, her wheels retracting, innocent and curious to see what we'd be learning today.

A hundred yards offshore, while I was checking to see if the oil temperature was coming up, she swung around into the wind, by herself, pivoting left no matter how hard I pushed full right rudder. That's when it occurred to me that wind might be a factor today. Puff doesn't turn into the wind on her own unless she's forced to do such a thing by a fairly strong gust.

I brought her back to a downwind heading with a burst of power, propeller-blast on her rudder, stronger than the wind, but she felt balanced on a knife-edge as we taxied, and the waves were getting higher, white foam on the back sides, and wind-streaks on the water.

That's how long it took me to realize this simple situation was not getting better it was getting worse, and it would continue to get worse the farther downwind we taxied. At that point I thought perhaps it would be best not to fly today. We could do it if we had to, if Lassie suddenly appeared with news that Timmy had fallen down the well, but Lassie was resting elsewhere and this was not a day for a training flight.

With that, I tapped the rudder to turn home. Puff instantly swung right, harsh into the wind. Except that she didn't make it round. She turned sideways to the storm, a gust punched beneath her upwind wing and burst upward. Silly me had turned to the right instead of to the left, so that my weight left of centerline was helping the wind roll us inverted.

I watched the left float plunge out of sight underwater; saw the wingtip follow.

Richard! The wind! Help!

Travels with *Puff*

I slammed all my weight down on the right rudder pedal, jammed the throttle forward to propeller-blast her tail to the left, pick that wing up, roll her back level.

It all went slow-motion, her wing under a thousand pounds of water.

So slowly, she came round … turned toward the wind, her sunken wing began to lift. One hard gust now, I thought, and I'll lose her. Puff's angels flashed against the storm to keep that from happening. Gradually her bow eased into the wind, her underwater wing lifted just clear of the deep and all at once her flight controls were working, as though we were flying in that wind. Turned back, headed the opposite direction, I could see the whitecaps I hadn't seen from the back side of the waves, felt Puff gasp for air.

Do we want to do this?

Puff was putting on her brave, but she had never dropped a wing into the lake before, and knew same as I did: if we had rolled another foot to the left there would have been a ton of water rushing into the cockpit through the open hatch, taking us under. (Her pilot hadn't thought to close the hatch in case such a thing might happen, another link in the chain he made this afternoon.)

She shook off the last quarter-ton of water and her fears soon as I agreed that we did not want to stay on the lake just now, and taxied shoreward, spray dashing over the windscreen with every wave she breasted.

Back on the beach, I allowed a windy de-briefing:

1. When the water looks not all that rough and you're on the upwind side of the lake, remember you're looking at the one calm patch the lake has to offer, every place else is disaster;

2. Might be well to check the aviation weather before taxiing out, just for fun. (When I checked it, sitting in the cockpit after engine shutdown and Puff asleep, the closest airport was calling winds at 15 gusting 23, peak gust 30 knots. Thirty-knot gusts is no time to be on the water in Light Sport Airplanes. Puff knows that, I know that;

3. If something's a little strange, the airplane spinning around into the wind on her own, wake up, pilot! She's reacting to what's going on in the air, not what you think isn't happening, in your mind;

4. Instead of contemplating how much water will be pouring into the airplane if that wing rolls deeper in the water, you might help her turn upwind, and slam that hatch shut while you're at it;

5. I earned my Captain Chicken membership by using good judgment to avoid bad situations before they got worse. I am not required to push the "before they get worse" part to the last possible second or until we're upside down in the water. Early decisions are good decisions.

There you have it. Not one minute in the air today, but we came closer to trouble than we did in four hours yesterday over swamps seething with alligators.

Captain Chicken lost a feather or two, but he's vowed to hold more tightly to the few he has left.

The only photo today is a word-video:

Imagine Puff tossed in a Perfect Storm as we see in the movies: lifted skyward one instant on giant foaming breakers, next plunged into the depths disappeared from sight, then inching up again, slowly, under the weight of green water over her bow, then rising at last, shaking free, plumes of spray thrown twenty, thirty feet over her rudder.

Imagine a supertanker in the same lake with Puff, fighting to stay afloat in those rogue waves and losing, distress rockets firing skyward, crew rushing for the lifeboats.

When you have that scene clear as terror your mind, then ease it back half a notch, and you have our day on the water. Yet it was not the waves but the wind, which nearly drowned us.

Last minute we had run for cover and we made it, barely, sea-drenched but alive.

Aside from that, not much happened today. Puff dripping wet, safe on the beach, I felt a wisp of a frown: if we have this much trouble on our home lake, what are we going to find in those 3,300 miles west?

Monster seas notwithstanding, if I've learned one lesson in all my days, it's this: *What scares more than dying by storm or mountain is being bored to death.*

Chapter 16

Flying Again!

The wind moved on this morning, having heard of a seaplane to the east that required harassing, and left Puff and me with a near-calm day.

I thought I needed to learn a little more about how she behaves during an engine failure after takeoff, so we did some pretend-failures over a nearby lake.

To hold one's airspeed after a power failure (and it's really important to hold one's airspeed), it's up to the pilot to push the control stick forward and turn his aircraft into a glider in fairly short order.

This is something that those who don't yet fly little airplanes sometimes forget … every airplane is a glider with an engine screwed on it. Just because the engine stops, it doesn't mean the airplane quits flying. What happens is that it glides smoothly down to land … that's why airplanes without engines (or with engines which have stopped) are called "gliders."

Engineless gliders are designed to take their time coming back to earth. Puff is not designed to take so long. That's why we practiced today—when the engine stops in the future neither of us will be terribly bothered, as we've been there done that, and all we need to do is find some water or a level place to land.

Puff's rate of descent today was between 700 and 800 feet per minute ... that is, from an altitude of 500 feet we had 40 seconds from the moment the engine quit until we touched the surface of the planet, which is a fairly long time. I could have extended that a bit by flying more slowly, but 'Rey pilots would be upset with me if I told you I established a glide speed less than our bulletproof 70 mph. All it takes is practice, knowing that she can stay in the air a little longer if one is careful, but we won't go there today.

I enjoy the quiet with the engine idling (later I'll do some practice with the propeller stopped), just the hush of the wind as we glide. Here's what it sounds like: (imagine the sound of wind blowing softly into a microphone, one breath for 40 seconds).

So you see an engine failure is no huge concern if you're practiced and ready when the propeller stops turning. One gets into trouble when one believes that engines never fail, and flies out of gliding distance from a reasonable place to land. Not always easy, but it's the pilot's job to consider such things.

You think I don't know what I'm doing, writing this little bit of technical flying stuff in a gentle-adventure book? I know what I'm doing. I'm chasing whatever little fears are left in our not-yet-pilot readers, I'm hinting about flying your own airplane, some day. The freedom and the beauty of flight are worth the study and practice they require, since even the practice is fun.

If I've learned one lesson in all my days, it's this: *We can never convince anyone to do what way deep down they don't already want to do.*

I worked with Puff for a while as she slept on the beach, making a head-rest, adjusting the seat attach fittings, putting fuel quantity numbers on the gage. In the midst of such pleasant work the song from *Oliver* appeared in my mind: *Where is Love?* It's a beautiful melody, a little wistful and melancholy, so why should it come to mind just now? Is it Puff singing, as she dreams? Maybe it's all in the title, to remind that Love isn't spacetime-bound. A philosophical question or a personal one for anyone who hums along? Haven't solved that one ... it's still playing in my mind as I write.

CHAPTER 17

"Routine Flight"

A s if there is such a thing. The purpose of any flight may sound routine: "Flight instruction," "Aircraft test flight," "To Sebring for engine maintenance," but the flying itself nearly always has some unexpected gift. Those can't-be-planned events filter into a pilot's life nearly every time she lifts off the ground, whether or not she makes a note of them in her logbook: "Cloud of flamingoes rose from the reeds."

Today's flight was the above, "To Sebring for engine maintenance," with Dan Nickens. He said he'd be flying over the house around 9:30 and did I want to join him on his trip?

Puff and I met Dan and Jennifer at 1,500 feet at 9:30, the air aloft still and smooth.

A lake appeared along the way ahead, Dan eased down from altitude and of course we followed. Dan's preferred cross-country cruising over water, natural for him, is at an altitude between zero and two feet. Puff and I were conservative, flying way up high at six feet to take a picture:

Here's this odd contrast once again about the man, one hour he's flying 80 mph, inches over the uncaring wavetops, the next I imagine him installed at the Club, wearing one of those jackets with suede at the elbows, discussing geological sediment layers, Pangaea and the structures of the Mid-Atlantic Ridge.

I smile at contrast like that, even when I don't have the courage to drop into proper formation with him at that altitude (wing-men usually fly lower than their leader's plane).

There's your routine flight: the surface whipping by, a sheet of night-blue lightning, the waterfall thunder from the engine a few feet behind the cockpit, the wind ripping curtains of hard fresh air inches from your face.

Dan has no lifetime guarantee on the engine he was bringing for inspection, I thought, watching Jennifer's keel touch a wave in a small cloud of spray. Do we? Do we come to earth with a lifetime guarantee?

Should you not be completely satisfied with this lifetime, dear mortal, you may choose an indefinite number of different lives, at no charge to yourself beyond your prepaid deposits of courage and humor.

I doubted the at no charge provision, as we do pay for our lifetimes not just with courage and humor but determination to live them as best we can, to our highest right. Yet never have I doubted that we can choose a different lifetime, after this one or before or in the very midst of our adventures.

If I've learned one lesson in all my days, it's this: *We can change lifetimes whenever we wish, by deciding we'll be different from who we were before.*

Thinking this, losing track of my altitude, Puff's keel touched the water at 80 mph, a quick sliding thud, bounced airborne again, an impact that brought me awake in a flash. I may have a lifetime guarantee, I thought, settling back up to my safe altitude of thirty-six inches, but I prefer to develop the life I've got all spread before me just now, thank you, before I plan the next.

CHAPTER 18

Sebring Encore

My task today was to fly the 60 miles south to Sebring, and for a change, do it way up at altitude. At one time in my life "at altitude" meant 38,000 feet with a cruise climb to 42,000, the sky all dark above, helmet visor down against the sun and the sound of oxygen hissing in my mask.

With Puff a few hours ago, "at altitude" was clear up to 1,500 feet on a hot hazy Florida afternoon, she liking the view from so high but not much caring for the turbulent up- and down-drafts, for she was traveling and not seeking lift. Soon as I turned on the camera to record the power of warm air rising, everything smoothed out. If you want to see 30 seconds of smooth air, I have it on video.

It was on the way back from Sebring, over the town of Frostproof, that I saw something I hadn't noticed in decades, something which struck my biplane passengers at once: "The farm, the town—they're toys!"

Perhaps we were at the perfect altitude, but Frostproof was laid out on kitchen-table Earth below us, all in miniature and astonishing detail. The grand homes, the trailer parks, the churches, even little cars rolling on streets you'd swear were real.

The dramas this moment, I thought, in every one of those houses below! In the bank and the church, in offices and shops and on the street, drama in progress, folks joyful and frightened, fatigued and inspired. Some crying this moment, some whistling. All the actors in place on their stage, each one living the script, speaking it perfectly without thinking what words come next.

For someone a thousand feet higher than we flew, there was even a toy SeaRey flying over the table, with a tiny pilot looking down from his windy open cockpit, a-wonder at so many scenes being played all at once. Their scenes, my scenes, all of us with a part that needs be played.

Flying will do that, from time to time, blind-side you with its literal perspective, pushes you into knowing none of it's real. Beyond each one of those chess-piece players, a different self hovers who lives beyond the set and the script and the drama, who cares only for the expressing of love—will my actor take the chance onstage to do that in this play, this episode, this lifetime?

Then Frostproof faded in the haze behind us, it was back to airspeed and altitude and fuel remaining, but not quite. The feeling, the connection with those lives flickered in and out after the town disappeared. I couldn't shake it out of my mind: in every single one of those toy houses: theater in progress, lessons being avoided, lessons being learned. Puff's and mine, too.

North of Lake Wales, the little airplane tugged me down, she wanted to land on the water and be still for a minute after being banged about in the sky. Which we did, choosing a lake as round and silver as a dollar in the sun. After we came to a stop on the waves, I reached my hand to the water gone silver to blue, cooler thicker wetter an arms-length from the cockpit than the air had been, a thousand feet up.

Then we were off again and before long home: sixty miles in sixty minutes. A flight in which Puff was passed on the road below not only automobiles, but by an 18-wheeler hauling an open trailer of oranges.

When she miffed at that, I reminded her that the truck likely was not free to take time for cooling off in any lake it wished.

If I've learned one lesson in all my days, it's this: *The skills and abilities we take for granted this minute, some others in the world would burst with joy, to have them for their own. As we would, sometimes to have theirs.*

CHAPTER 19

Technical Matters

*I*t does. One needs to know what one's airplane will do and what she won't. That means becoming one's own test pilot, when what one needs to know isn't printed.

Can Puff, for instance, can she taxi through a sea of lily pads and take off again?

I went straight to the source, and asked her. "Lily pads a problem, Puff?"

Let's don't do the lily pads.

"We've never done lily pads. They'll be fun to taxi through, and pretty!"

I'd prefer not.

"Oh, come on!"

If you insist. You're the pilot.

I didn't catch the warning in her voice. In the future I will listen for *You're the pilot.*

So began my lilypad/takeoff folly:

For some reason, I elected to taxi into the sea of lilypads at fairly high speed, and so in order to keep from embedding us in the beach, I had to add power and rudder to bend the turn sharp enough to clear the shore.

Back on open water, I pushed the throttle to full power, "OK, Puff, let's fly!"

I heard the full power of the engine, and I heard her response:

Let's what?

None of her glad dash for the sky, she was heavy and dull. Could it have something to do, I thought, with the lilypads?

That's when we headed for shore. In a minute we were beached, engine silent, Puff asleep.

I stepped out of the airplane into the alligator-infested water, waded to the tail. And you know what? Lilypads. We had harvested 30 pounds of lilypads, which are neither streamlined when clumped in a bunch around one's tailpost nor much designed for flight. Aerodynamic as a sack of potatoes and just as heavy, it would have been as pilots like to say somewhat challenging if Puff had agreed to fly, her center of gravity dragged way into the Danger Do Not Fly zone.

Lily pads cleared, alligators dodged, I started her engine and we turned for open water.

Thank , you.

Crisp and formal. No I told you, or Next time you might try listening to me before you insist on trouble. Just the one word, the pause for the comma and the other: *Thank , you.*

For two hours we flew shallow-water landings, weaving high-speed among islands of reeds, practiced short-field landings, obstacle takeoffs, full-stall-and-broad-slide quickstops.

On the way home, quiet cruise a thousand feet in the air, I sensed she was looking to the horizon west.

What's out there?

She whispered, she who knew only flatlands, rivers and lakes and swamps and most of her life with me.

"Space or time, Puff, geography or adventure? It's a big world, both ways."

We're almost ready, aren't we?

"Another week and we're on our way."

Not time. I mean you and me. We're getting to know each other, aren't we, we're ready for what's out there?

"Step by step, Puff, there's not a whole lot we won't be able to handle. Patience. A long crosscountry flight is fifty short ones."

Ah. Thank you.

There was no comma between the words.

CHAPTER 20

Powers of Truth

O n the private website for SeaRey builders and flyers, there was a post last night which was a warning, too. The warning was be careful when the engine fails, since from an altitude of a thousand feet, the post-writer's airplane was unable to make one complete circle before it was on the ground.

He didn't go into much detail, so I assumed his airplane was heavier than is Puff, his turn may have been different than I would fly. It didn't feel to me as if Puff would be so unforgiving. An F-84F or a Boeing 737, I'd agree, but Puff? It was hard to sleep, thinking she might be keeping a secret from me.

This morning, preflight inspection complete, I started her engine and she came awake, splashing carefree into the lake.

In a few seconds, she slowed.

Something wrong?

"Oh, thinking about the comment ..."

Of course she knew which comment, as her spirit's linked with mine when she's awake.

Not you and me, about that can't-turn business. Not true for us.

As if that were the end of the story, case closed where shall we be flying today.

"Why's it true for him, then," I said, "and his airplane?"

I'm not psychic, Richard.

Puff turned into the wind on the water.

She's a heavy airplane? Too much drag at idle? She's flying too big a circle? Where are we going today?

"I don't doubt you, Puff, but he's talking SeaRey and you're SeaRey, too. How come you're so sure?"

How come you're sure you can ride a bicycle? You just . . . you know you can. I can do two circles, power off, from a thousand feet. Just because it's true for him and his airplane, doesn't mean it's true for us!

"Would you mind . . ."

Of course I'll show you. That's what these days are for, you said. See what we can do together and what we can't. I'll show you. Two turns from a thousand feet.

"Can you do two turns from a hundred feet?"

Oh, you like to test me.

"I'm only . . ."

Of course I can.

"Puff you're . . ."

. . . but I'll need a little power.

Note to self: Puff never says can't.

A few minutes later we were a thousand feet above the lake, Puff pretending to be disinterested.

I pulled the power to idle, lowered her nose and began the turn. If words were video, you'd see we were still a couple hundred feet in the air by the time she finished two full turns.

If I've learned one lesson in all my days, she said, *it's this: True for others isn't true for me.*

We landed on a lake by a restaurant, around noon, and a small crowd came out to tell me how pretty she is.

We choose our truth, I thought, by what we can demonstrate to ourselves.

Pretty she is, and smart.

CHAPTER *21*

Sand and
Sea and Sky

We're sand-grains in an hour-glass. That's the way it feels today, sand in the upper half of the glass, feeling the event-horizon moving on a different dimension beneath us, knowing there's gonna be a big change soon.

Today began with a purpose: time to be on our way, to fly north to the SeaRey factory, solve a few problems before the adventure's on us. Puff felt a little solemn, the way she does before a new unknown.

I called Dan before we left the lake, arranged to meet him in the air, though today he'd be flying the company's showcase demonstration aircraft.

How do we find each other, when there's a whole sky to hide in? Here's how it goes: just the same as we find each other in the midst of lifetimes, broadcasting our position on secret channels:

"Hi Papa Echo," Dan's voice on the radio. "Sierra Romeo here, do you read?" (The company SeaRey's N-number ends in "SR", and Dan's transmitting without knowing whether I can hear him or not. If not, his only answer is silence ... we could be anywhere, or our radio not working, no clue to him that we're even in the air.)

"Hi Sierra Romeo. Papa Echo's five miles south of Clermont, north-bound." (The biggest question answered … now we know we're sharing the airspace. Even though we can't see each other, we will soon.)

"Sierra Romeo's five north of your position at one thousand five. Let's meet over the middle of the big lake; I'll need to land there."

"Roger. Papa Echo's at a thousand feet, looking." I chose a lower altitude than Dan's until I had his airplane in sight—sighting a tiny dot from miles away is easier when one chooses a background of sky instead of the cluttery camouflage of ground. How life in the air mirrors life on earth, as well!

Then silence, and scanning, scanning, somewhere out there … a dot! A dot circling, not moving straight-line direct, the way Dan would be flying now.

The dot's a buzzard, climbing in lift.

Another dot northward, heading south, sense of purpose.

"Papa Echo's got you in sight." It could have been a different aircraft I saw, but the chance of that is low, and at our closing speed I'll be seeing detail soon. Soon as the form takes shape, the strange capacity of humans to identify and connect works like oiled lightning. A few pixels and it's done: seems like a high wing, an upswept tail, a boat in the sky … identified! This is the one I'm looking for.

From that horizon of emptiness appeared at last what I was hoping to find, and now nothing else matters. Turn to intercept, get closer in the quickest safest way.

"Got you in sight, Papa Echo." Now it's mutual. An agreement to fly together.

It's all done with turns, angles, judgings of distance and speed, climb and power and rates of closure. Meeting someone we care about, in the air or on the ground, is infinitely complex, yet we go by what feels right to do, moment to moment, and things work out.

"Wheels up for a water landing." His airplane slowed, dropped down-ward. Puff and I did the same, power back, turning into the wind, and before long comes that familiar sound of a lake brushing against the hull, each of our airplanes slowing, floating on water now, instead of air.

I watched SR's landing gear come down, brief flags of white water alongside, then the wheels gone out of sight beneath the surface, feeling for the beach.

Touch of a switch, and Puff's wheels splash and disappear, as well. The rest is easy, a burst of power and the two aircraft are supported now by firm sand below instead of air or water. Like their pilots, the seaplanes are at home in many dimensions, we shift from one to another with hardly a thought.

Within minutes we were off again, switching surface from sand to water to air, flying together in a new direction, purpose shared.

We stopped briefly at Dan's hangar, at the end of his own ramp. "There are lily pads," he had said. "Take them slowly, you'll glide over." Then he added, "The ramp's steep, so keep your power on. And there's an eighty-degree turn at the top ... ."

Oh, my, I thought, La Rampa del Muerte, Parte Dos.

"You'll do fine." He was right, but would I accept his comment before I had proven it for myself? Not hardly. Doesn't happen often, that I'll accept "You'll do fine" before I've already done it.

Not a word from Puff, not a care that we might crash, and sure enough, she rolled up Dan's ramp, made the turn with ease, taxied to his hangar.

Later, time to fly away, Dan asked some strange questions. "Puff's brakes OK?"

"Brakes are good. Why?"

"Her tailwheel steering's working?"

"Working well. Are you trying to frighten me?"

"Oh no," he said. "You just want to take it slow going down the ramp, and come out of that last turn and into the water as straight as you can."

Neither Puff nor I worried—all the maneuvering went well, though her brakes weren't ready for so steep a ramp and we sort of rushed into the water a bit out of control. I saw what Dan meant, though ... take that steep ramp too fast into deep water, I thought, you can break an airplane in half.

Puff smiled at the thought: *Break in half, ha-ha. Not me.*

We arrived at the Progressive Aerodyne factory lake in the first minutes that the new ramp, the erstwhile Rampa del Diablo, was rebuilt and open for business once more.

Easy to power up that ramp today, when it had been beyond my skills last time I tried.

Now Puff was home again, and Kerry changed from dock-installer to airplane therapist. We talked for a while as he came up with solutions for her few low-grade fevers. Tomorrow we get serious about getting her ready for the big journey.

If I've learned one lesson in all my days, it's this: *Life starts new, every sunrise.*

CHAPTER 22

Puff and the President

A irplanes do not complain. Sometimes things are not quite as right as they could be, but Puff is no exception—her life is flying and if she has problems she will fly anyway, or do her best to fly unless her pilot ties thirty pounds of lily-pads to her tail and says go for it she might say go for what.

Today at the factory she slept though the repairing of her fuel system, the alignment of her tires and the fixing of her sliding canopy so that it works as smoothly as designed.

What made today interesting was that from 10 am till 7 pm, it was Kerry Richter, the designer of the SeaRey and president of the company, who came out in the heat of the hangar bay and personally resolved her problems, one after another.

Here he is sighting down the canopy track, which was bent and which he removed and replaced, then solved a series of connected problems through the next several hours.

As well, he replaced the wheel bearings and took business calls while operating drill motors and rivet guns.

If you brought your Cessna or Beechcraft in for maintenance, chances are the shop would have closed at 4:30 and you'd be dragged off to your motel for the next 16 hours.

I've chatted from time to time about the close family of pilots and owners of this airplane that Kerry brought to life. One of them told me that it's good that he isn't the chief financial officer, as the company would go broke with the man giving away his time for free to customers with troubles to be solved.

Is this the source of that family's feeling for each other, their willingness to help … did it start on a day like today with this guy going out of his way to improve the life of one of his aircraft?

Chapter 23

I Laugh at Thunderstorms

orecast: thunderstorms. Ha-ha, I thought, for the morning was bright and clear, the wind light, perfect for flying.

Dan and I were at the factory early, he to fly a demonstration flight for a potential SeaRey customer, me to finish the last details of Puff's tune-up at Progressive Aerodyne and to watch Kerry Richter take her up on his own, to see that she was perfectly rigged and fit.

Kerry changed the pitch of the propeller ever so slightly, that she might fly faster than she has been flying, at the price of adding another second to two to her takeoff time.

What a strange feeling, watching her taxi down the ramp and into the water—my lady going to dance with another guy.

As Kerry has more SeaRey experience than anyone in the world, however, I allowed as their dance would be fine with me—she's dancing with her father.

I said that several times to myself, "It's fine with me," as I watched Puff and Kerry race high-speed around the far edge of the lake, spray like rainbows flying in the sunlight behind them. Then they were aloft, and I smiled at how quiet the sound of her overhead, more a whispery whir from her propeller than the heavy beat of a conventional airplane engine.

They disappeared for fifteen minutes or so, then returned from altitude, power back into a long glide, the faintest whistle now alongside the whir, an altogether pleasant sound. A perfect landing (that is, one with not the slightest bounce on touchdown), and in two minutes they were back. Kerry shut down the engine, Puff asleep at once.

"She's a good-flying airplane!" He was out of the cockpit, found a socket drive, an end-wrench. "Just a little bit out of trim, so we'll fix that …"

He applied the wrench to the linkage of her right flap, then adjusted the right aileron pushrod a fraction of an inch. "I think we might have picked up another five miles per hour." He put the wrenches away. "She's a good airplane," he said again. "Go take her up, see what you think of her now."

Next minute it was Puff and me together again skimming the water at the far end of the lake, in a high-speed turn to takeoff, bright flashes on the ripples blurring to sun-color streaks as we lifted from the water.

Out of sight from the ground, out over a round plain of water south, we practiced familiar steps, slow flight at 40 mph, then extreme slow flight at full power and 26. Stalls flaps up and flaps down, power off and power … not many airplanes won't stall with full power, the SeaRey is one of them. Puff hangs on her propeller at an impossible steep angle, a gymnast with a move all her own, gaining altitude every minute.

In level flight at all cruise powers she was indeed moving faster by five miles per hour. She felt light and trim, warmed-up and happy in her sky. Her words in my mind:

I like me! I like the new me! I'm the real me, a little more.

Her words trailed off in happiness. Of course, I thought. The more we're able to move to match our spirit, the more we're expressing our true being, in whatever world we find ourselves.

Travels with *Puff*

We tried some more moves of the dance and all went well. Then we were whirring down the edge of silence to the water, whispering along the surface, lifting to the new ramp, water pouring away as she rose.

Kerry interpreted my delight with his work as he's been interpreting other pilots' pleasure for his airplane over the 20 years since the first SeaRey … screen out the fantastics and wonderfuls and thankyouKerrys and find the center: is your airplane flying the way you want it to fly, does it need further refining, any slight adjustment, another degree of trim, a few more revolutions per minute?

I stuffed the nylon bags of Puff's tools and accessories, left the factory and followed Dan as he flew a newly finished customer's airplane a few miles to Tavares for fuel and lunch. Then we were off south, for our Florida home, Dan flying formation alongside.

So far it had been me as wingman and Dan as leader, this was Puff's first time leading a flight of two. The best wingman stays in position behind and below the leader, and get this: no matter what the leader does, and without a word spoken unless in answer to the leader's comment or question.

Between me and Puff, then, we managed to give Dan some formation practice, suddenly turning away from his airplane, turning toward her, climbing, diving, slow-flying, power-changing. We found a lake along the way.

"Wheels are up for a water landing," I called on the radio.

"Two," he replied, that being his number in the flight and the only word necessary for me to know that he understood what we were about to do. We half-circled down to touch the water, Puff first and Dan's plane a second later, turned and made a takeoff, side by side.

Then we were turning to land at our home lake. We slid to rest on the water, the two airplanes idling ahead.

"I'll be on my way," he called. "Make it home before the thunderstorms."

"Good flight, Dan," I said.

Then he was off in a cloud of spray, northbound.

We taxied to our beach, Puff and I, lifted out of the water onto sand. "Thank you, Puff," I said aloud. No answer, but I knew she was one happy airplane, and I shut her engine down.

I enjoyed the silence for a while, reached for the logbook and filled in one more line with one more flight. Then I was out of the airplane, setting chocks under her wheels, tying her down wings and tail.

The sky was moderately dark with cloud, but the wind was gentle and the lake smooth. I walked to the house, wondering what I would write for the journal today, looked in the refrigerator ...

It almost never happens that I hear Puff when her engine's still. What I'm writing, it's strange but it happened, Puff's voice in my mind: *Richard, come quick, I'm scared!*

That's odd, I thought. I'll be right there, I thought, but first I'll look at the radar weather to see ... There were red-and-yellow fires, thunderstorms pouring over the screen, some nearly on us. How did this happen so fast?

I was out the door at once, the wind kicking whitecaps on the lake. Puff's streamers flying, she was trembling on her wheels in the wind. I slid her hatches tight shut, grabbed her canopy and engine covers, struggled in wind to fit them in place, the securing straps blown from my hands time and again. I quick tied the rudder lock in place as the first big drops of storm thudded down. How could this be happening so fast? It was only minutes ago the lake was calm as toast.

I grabbed a second set of tiedown straps, webbed them around the wing strut fittings, pulled them tight.

I'm frightened. The wind ...

Not to worry, Puff, I thought to her. You're double-tied, hatches closed, covers in place, controls locked, chocks in. Angled downhill, it'll take a tornado to break you loose.

Last year, remember the tornado?

It had crumpled airplanes like a writer's failed pages, scattered on the floor.

Not this year, Puff. Not now. This is a simple Florida thunderstorm.

The far side of the lake burst with light, count two and fresh sharp thunder struck us both, and a sheet, a whipping wet storm of rain, fierce heavy stinging drops.

It's OK, Puff. Our first thunderstorm! Isn't it fun?

No! Not fun! Am I all right, please?

You're fine. We need the rain, helps fill the lake. The wetland plants and creatures need it, too.

It was my first thunderstorm too, first in years, and I had forgotten how violent an everyday storm can be. Still it would take a monster something to pry Puff loose. I was a little scared, too.

The downburst soaked me through in seconds, glad I was for the water-proof camera case as I took pictures which don't begin to show how hard was the rain, but for those few unnatural streaks slashing across the image. It felt infinitely wetter and harder than the photo.

In a minute, a tentative voice:

I think I can enjoy this …

One third true from my airplane, I thought, two thirds courage in the face of what she could not change.

Ah, humans, I thought, and those whom they love.

CHAPTER 24

The Best Laid Schemes of Mice

It was a fine outline for the day: up for some serious flight testing of Puff and her new performance and speed from her factory tune-up, her old numbers gone obsolete. Then perhaps, condition permitting, we do a little soaring in the afternoon lift. That'll be fun to fly ... what kind of lift will we find, what rate of climb will we have in a big thermal, being lifted skyward, power off?

By morning, the wind was kicking up on the lake, 15 mph with gusts to 20. Our plans for water-flying were cracked, with gusts to broken asunder. No matter, there are a few small items to attend to—change the tailwheel bearing, some last touches on the sliding canopy hatch.

Then the call from a friend, did I know about the big hailstorm forecast for this afternoon, the sustained winds?

Big Hailstorm?

As the Scarecrow loved fire, as the Tin Man loved rain, as the Wicked Witch loved having pails of water thrown upon her, so do little airplanes love hailstorms. Big Hailstorms reduce them to wreckage in the blink of an eye do I know about the big hailstorm. Yes, as a matter of fact, I do, now.

Puff was trapped on shore. The wind tearing whitecaps from the waves, she stood unprotected on her beach. Yet not a sound did I imagine from her, she slept serenely. I had the sense that she had put her blind faith in me, trusting I'd do whatever was best to save her life.

Across the lake stood the giant hangars of Kermit Weeks' Fantasy of Flight, filled with his rare old airplanes. All I'd have to do for her safety would be to sail Puff into the wind to Kermit's seaplane ramp, come up from the water, taxi to his hangar and pound on the door till someone might give the waifs shelter from the looming violence.

For powerful liability reasons, I knew that my friend does not allow other aircraft in his hangars. I called anyway.

"Kermit, you know the storm ... ?"

"Huge! I was watching the radar. You'd better bring Puff over now, Richard, let's put her in the big hangar."

"I can't tell you how much I appreciate ..."

"It's no problem. Wind's coming up. Better bring her over now."

I was down to the beach at once, setting loose her covers and control locks and tiedown straps. The wind whipped over us both, she tilted left-right on her wheels.

Everything's going to be all right, I thought, only half a mile of water to cross. Just don't you dare let the wind get sideways under one wing, I thought, don't you dare. Or we'll capsize together in the middle of the lake and that would be ... that would be unacceptable.

I pulled the chocks from her wheels and settled into the cockpit. Master switch ON, boost pump ON, choke ON, Mag 2 switch OFF, throttle Idle.

Keep her pointing into the wind, Richard. Everything will be fine.

"Prop clear!"

Starter key to START, Puff blinked awake, her engine firing at once. Mag 2 switch ON. Oil pressure coming up, choke OFF, throttle up before the engine dies.

Puff slipped into the water, not a question, not a word. If my pilot says we're going through the whitecaps, we're going through the whitecaps.

Wheels UP, and we gained a little speed into the wind.

If I were Kerry Richter, I thought, would I push the power and step-taxi highspeed over the waves? No. He'd say there's no need to go slamming through the whitecaps, stressing the airplane, when slicing through them one by one will get us there just as well.

Travels with *Puff*

Except it gets us there slower. The windscreen went squirrely in shredded waves bursting up from the bow. I could make out the far shore through the glass, but not much else. Wouldn't it be nice to take a picture of what I see right now. Yes it would be nice, no I won't be taking pictures I have other matters on my mind just now.

A quarter of the way across. No turning back, don't even think about turning out of the wind.

Half-way across, I remembered Kermit's fence, set between the lakeshore and the runway, to keep cattle from straying into the way of landing aircraft. There was a gate for cows in the fence. There was not a gate for airplanes.

If we taxied up the ramp, there'd be no way we could get to the hangar, and Puff would be as vulnerable to the storm as though she had never left the beach. Worse, as I had left her tiedown anchors on the beach.

We'd have to fly, to get over the fence, onto the runway.

Turning back was out of the question. Offer one wing to the wind, she'd be on her back and sinking in seconds ... there shall be no turns.

We'll fly.

Wheels are UP for a water takeoff. Flaps are full DOWN for most lift in the rough water, boost pump is ON. Here we go, Puff.

I caught myself, and paused. I hadn't fastened my seat belt or shoulder harness, sure that we'd be not flying but taxiing. The belts clicked into place.

Rough water takeoff, here we come. Yet as we neared the upwind edge of the lake, the water went smoother, the whitecaps gone. In fact, a hundred yards ahead the water was nearly calm, it hadn't felt the wind tearing on it long enough to build waves. This might be one wild crosswind takeoff, Puff, but at least there'd be no pounding to bits in our immediate future.

We taxied through waves going smaller every minute, reached the smooth windy east side. Follow the shoreline for a curving crosswind take-off, be ready for wild turbulence and sudden flying sideways the instant the wind catches us in the air. From then it's simple ... climb a few hundred feel, circle and land on Kermit's long grass runway heading straight into the wind, then taxi carefully crosswind to that giant hangar and safety.

Here we go, Puff, piece of cake.

She wasn't nearly so stressed as I, since she believed what I said about the cake.

Full throttle, and seconds later she was on the step, then off the water and climbing. Her wings slammed hard to the right in the hammer of boiling wind over the trees at the shoreline, we slid sideways more than straight ahead.

The little seaplane clawed half a thousand feet upward, turned to parallel the grass runway. Visitors to Fantasy looked up through the air … what's that boat doing in the sky, and in this wind?

I touched the gear switch. "Wheels are DOWN for a land landing," I said aloud, checked flaps and boost pump, trimmed Puff to fly her smoothest. Faced into the wind near the ground, she was moving less than 20 mph over the grass when we touched. We spent quite some time taxiing crosswind to the hangar. Shielded finally by the mass of Kermit's monster building, I shut the engine down and Puff, no stress, her trust in me now strong and sure, fell fast asleep.

I pushed her into the silent cavern of the place, floor clean as a dinner-plate, found a Puff-size open space at the edge and parked her there.

Not long after, Kermit arrived, intent on moving his huge B-25

inside, too. Hail won't destroy a warplane, but it can cause big damage to metal skin and Plexiglass.

Puff and I didn't get any new performance numbers today and we didn't go soaring. We racked up a total of three minutes' flying.

As I write, it is five hours later. The Big Hailstorm hasn't showed, or at least not yet, it hasn't. Puff, as Kermit put it, is visiting the Aero Club, surrounded by aircraft with endless stories to tell. She's parked by the wing of a Curtiss P-40 Warhawk, by the nose of a North American P-51 Mustang, the tail of a Supermarine Spitfire, her other wing by a Grumman Avenger torpedo plane.

Travels with *Puff*

Across the way, facing her, a 1911 Curtiss pusher, next a 1918 Sopwith Snipe, a Consolidated B-24 Liberator bomber and a Grumman Duck amphibian biplane. The wide tail structure of the B-25 towers over her cockpit.

Mouse-like she seems, the smallest lightest civilianest plane in that vast hangar. She'll stay there till Monday, as more storms are forecast. My guess is that she'll be hearing a story or two about the days, long before she was born, yet from which she has come.

I'll disagree with Robert Burns' poem. The best-laid schemes of mice and men, they don't go oft astray. If I've learned one lesson in all my days, it's this: *What seems like disaster, it's the unexpected touch of our own destiny.*

CHAPTER 25

Way Quiet Today

Puff came out of Kermit's Aero Club two days later, unscratched by storms, but not herself ... dazed.

We taxied the long way to the end of the grass runway, but she said not a word, not a thought-picture about her time with the warplanes. I sensed her silence was out of courtesy: If You Don't Have Anything Kind to Say, Say Nothing.

Do warplanes have their own Post Traumatic Stress Disorder, either from their service in battle or from missing the battles they were built to fight? I imagined living through a 2 a.m. flak-and-bombs thunderstorm with a bunch of PTSD'd warplanes and had a guess why my little seaplane didn't get much rest, even with her engine shut down and cold.

Puff, who doesn't know what war is, or why, went silent amid the war stories, and stayed silent even as we were ready for takeoff.

The wind was straight down the grass, and before I had the throttle pushed full open she was flying, anxious to get away. An awkward two-minute flight to our home lake, a water landing close to protected shores while a strange wind whisked the deeper parts of the lake into dark swirls of lion's-paw wavelets. A stiff breeze, yet not a whitecap in sight.

Up on her beach and tied down, she was instantly asleep, not a word to say.

I had hoped to do some flying, but felt as oddly uncomfortable with the wind as Puff had felt with her military companions.

There was no reason not to fly ... perhaps a little, as the wind was gusting to 20 mph. That much wind I can work with on land, and I feel Puff's confident there, too, but our limits are closer on the water and nobody's comfortable on the edge of limits. A seaplane pilot told me once, early on, "Landplane pilots have their worries, but sinking is not one of them."

Most of all though, was this eeriness not about the wind but about those hours we were apart. Puff and I didn't connect today, for some reason she was no more speaking to me than she was to the warbirds in the Aero Club. I'm grateful to Kermit Weeks for giving her shelter, even if my airplane can't at the moment acknowledge the same.

The rest of the day I tinkered with little things—tailwheel didn't need new bearings after all; fixed the headrest; practiced loading most everything that'll be going with us on the trip. Maybe the trouble's just that it's been too long, three days now with barely a few minutes in the air.

Or not. Has she suddenly realized that I was a military pilot, once, and now all of a sudden I'm a bad guy? Must my friendship with Puff go through every analog to a human relationship, including odd estrangements, communication shutdowns, misunderstandings?

I'm glad for the miasma. It happens almost never, and now that it has, it'll be the last miasmafication ever ... over, done, moving ahead.

Come on, tomorrow.

CHAPTER 26

The Day After

For the last fifty years, since I resolved to trust my own perceptions, I've known that airplanes have spirits. The startlingest example then, I wrote in a story called *Steel, Aluminum, Nuts and Bolts,* now chapter something in *A Gift of Wings.* It's still a wonder to me; true story.

Enter Puff the SeaRey, half a century later. My touch with her is the first time I've had a long-term ongoing conversation with a flying machine, a connection expressed in feeling-pictures, turned to words. I'm not surprised or wondering when I feel her comments in my mind. What follows are not her words but mine, to share the way of talking that's grown between us.

That had grown between us until yesterday, when she returned from two nights' storm refuge at the Aero Club, the hangar filled with warplanes.

She came away unspeaking from her shelter in that giant place. Had I asked her what was wrong, I think she would have said, *Oh, nothing …*

I didn't ask but got the same feeling, that a chasm had opened between us. It lasted all day and night, nothing could close it but a shift in our earth.

Hoping as always for the best, wishing it had blown away with yesterday's Wind from the Dark Places, I untied the little seaplane, made my preflight inspection, rolled her to the water and started the engine.

"Good morning, Puff."

She crept into the lake without her usual happy splash.

You are who you are now.

"You mean we're not who we used to be, any more," I said, then understood what she meant.

You were a fighter pilot. With guns. With bombs and rockets. You were a destroyer.

"I flew between wars, Puff. I didn't kill anybody."

You would have.

"Back then, I don't know. I probably would have." I wanted to believe the *I don't know* was truer than the *probably would have.*

You wouldn't do that now?

"No, I wouldn't. It was long ago. There's a reason why fighter pilots are kids."

You are who you are now. You're not who you were then.

"Oh," I said. "In the night, in the hangar with the warplanes, you found out your pilot whom you trusted every minute till now, he's a destroyer."

You're not who you were.

"Puff, I was a kid. I wanted to fly! I believed what they told me to believe. Defend your country! Be a fighter pilot!"

You were there. Would you have ... If they said ... would you have ...?

"Puff, you're right. I'm not who I was then. If I could talk with that kid ... do you know how many times I've tried getting through to him, in his flight suit and his G-suit and blind unthinking pride, his trust in the word of a senior officer who was just the next kid in line?"

Did you? Did you get through?

"Some versions of him, I got through. One of them, later on, is me." This was not a comfortable conversation, blue water turning to snowdrops splashing at her bow. Can we talk about something else, Puff?

One of them is you.

"Those warplanes with you in the hangar, they weren't jets, were they? They weren't what I flew."

You know that. It went round the hangar, all night long. Mustang about "Double-ya double-wa Two." Raids and strikes and battles. Spitfire called it "The Big Show." But it wasn't a show. They were killing airplanes. Other things, too, and people, but they were killing airplanes!

"They believed it had to be done, Puff, or the earth would be a slave camp. It was war as the world had never lived, their back was to the wall, the airplanes and the humans who loved them. They believed they were fighting for a future. And that future included little seaplanes flying free in the sun, touching down on hidden lakes. The future they believed in is you!"

They believed. Was it true?

"That time, best I can tell, they were right. It's so much easier for us mortals to kill strangers than to care for them, particularly when we're frightened and convinced it's not us going to die, but them."

The warplanes. Every night, they talk about what happened, a whole history ago, hour on hour, and it's all destroying!

"Do you know how many warplanes were built, Spitfires and Mustangs and Thunderbolts?"

Hundreds.

"Tens of thousands, many tens of thousands were built, and flew into air battles, year after year. Do you know how many are left?"

No.

"Maybe fifty Mustangs, a dozen Spitfires. Maybe three Messerschmitts, ten Hurricanes. A few others. The rest are gone, the tens of thousands. Crashed. Lost at sea. Shot down. Blown up midair."

I wondered about that. Are the spirits of aircraft the same as ours? If Puff's chosen her airplane-body as I've chosen my human-body, is her spirit as ongoing as mine?

"They're gone, all those fighter-plane bodies and their pilots-in-bodies and their futures that could have been. They're gone because humans must have leaders, and leaders demand power and power is useless to leaders unless it can rule and dominate, unless it can destroy."

You're a human.

"I'm no leader, Puff. If I were, I'd demand the power to control, to force and finally to kill. Political leaders, religious leaders, they're desperate for ..."

Richard, stop!

I blinked. Our friendship changes, this kind of talk.

"Ah, Puff, I'm sorry. I have my dark places, don't I?"

Maybe last time I was a Spitfire. This time I'm a seaplane, and I'll be the best seaplane I can be.

I sensed her smile.

I may need your help with that.

Airplane humor. To be her best, she'll need my help for sure.

And then, an odd moment, I saw behind her smile: I'll need her help, too, to be the best human I can be.

Where are we off to today?

She, descendent of destroyers and of savers of life, me the same, choosing our direction now, as we do every moment.

If I've learned one lesson in all my days, it's this: *We change. We're not who we were.*

"North," I said. "Let's try north, see what we need to learn today."

North we flew.

CHAPTER 27

A Day for Soaring

lmost dead calm, this morning, the lake become mirror of a cloud-less sky.

Since the beach angles down into the water, I need only untie the little seaplane, toss her wheel-chocks out of the way, and she'll roll on her own to the water.

Today I practiced wearing hiking boots into the water, and stepped from the lake into Puff's cockpit. If that works, it'll save carrying an extra pair of shoes on the long voyage; every pound counts. (Note from my near future, that is, me-now, as I write: The boots won't work, in the water. After a few hours in wet boots, one wishes they were dry.)

Engine started, Puff was awake and curious, yesterday's stress become water under her hull.

We're going soaring, aren't we?

She purred along, a boat carrying the modest weight of her wings, knowing that before long she'd be wings carrying the modest weight of a boat, and that it was all right with her if I was feeling technical.

A touch of power, spray flashing briefly alongside, fountains of diamonds in sunlight. Simple as that, she had cast away from the planet yet again, and we were free in the sky.

"Here's the game, Puff. We're at a thousand feet, we can use only a little power, pretend we're a glider at min sink."

"V min sink," is air-talk for the velocity at which an airplane descends as slowly as possible in still air.

For Puff, min sink is 55 mph. We held that speed, engine running softly at low power. We hunted rough air, sought the biggest bumps we could find, without much luck. A little lift here, a little there, enough to take us up, circling, to 1,500 feet, then a downdraft and we lost the altitude we gained.

This is hard. It's hard to climb when there's no lift.

Of course, I thought, we can always use more engine power.

That's cheating.

The land looked so pretty, wide green deserted pastures below, that I wanted to see if they were as smooth up close as they seemed from the air. I pushed the control stick forward, distracting Puff from lift-finding, and we swooped down to look at the grass. It was landable, all right, smooth and level and far from civilization.

Then Whoof!, struck by our own express elevator, Puff's wings shaking. Lift! We held min sink and up we went, circling, shuddering in the power of the air, 1,100 feet per minute on our rate of climb gage. The thermal topped out at 2,500 feet, her new altitude record.

Now she's asleep under her covers, dreaming of adventure tomorrow.

I haven't mentioned that we leave for Seattle on Sunday.

CHAPTER 28

Meeting Grandma Cat

A t first she was alone, Catalina and her memories:
    Then a sound coming close, a tiny propeller whirring, a small
    voice: Granma?

"Those were different times, Little One, difficult times. Long before you were born."

"Our mission was to find them when they bailed out, when their planes crashed into the sea, saving their pilots. Can you imagine how small is a man adrift on a raft, in the South Pacific Ocean?"

"When I came alongside his raft, he shouted, 'I LOVE YOU, CAT!'"

"We were sixteen of us, then. We flew all day, every day. They're gone now, the others—shot down, crashed, storms. I'm the only one left. I talk with them, sometimes."

"The Nancy Boats, the Clipper Ships, they're with me. And I'll be with you, Puff."

"Call in the dark, in your nights. When you're afraid, or alone. Know I'm with you, and I am."

"Never forget, Little Puff. As you are more than metal and fabric, so is your pilot more than flesh and bone. You are both of you spirit."

"My wings are over you now, and wherever you fly."

I'll remember, Granma Cat! I'll remember.

Travels with *Puff*

Chapter 29

First Day, and a Splash-In

P uff took fifteen seconds to lift from the water this morning, a long takeoff slide, loaded as she was with tools and spare parts and survival kit plus me and fuel and water to drink, peanuts and Oreo cookies, sunglasses and hat and goodbye home beach, home lake, home house.

We leveled a thousand feet above the ground, the first wisps of cloud marking the morning thermals, the air a clear river pouring by. I like flying with the canopy open, this option for air unconditioning standard with SeaReys at no extra cost.

Heading 010 degrees for half an hour, the radio filled with chatter from seaplanes at the Splash-In at Tavares. Someone called from a few miles south, "Is anybody using any kind of pattern there today?"

The pilot got no reply, which means, "Hey, it's a big lake. If you feel like flying a traffic pattern, fly one." As with most callings, the practical world of flying is different from what they teach in school.

The water was mostly calm; we landed on a patch with a few wind-ruffles, taxied high speed to the ramp, found it packed with seaplanes and visitors. I picked a weedy area along the shore instead, and Puff nosed in. The reeds were so thick that she stopped as though she had touched a beach.

(View from cockpit after parking in only space left at Splash-In. Park here free.)

I shut her engine down, stepped out of the cockpit into three feet of reeds and water.

I set the anchor for a tiedown, "Now you stay here, Puff," I thought.

Ha-ha, she muttered in her sleep.

I walked with the crowd around the seaplanes. Of the fifteen airplanes there at the moment, nine were SeaReys.

It was a successful Splash-In, beautiful aircraft on display in America's Seaplane City. We stayed a while, then nosed out of the foliage and took off for Dan Nickens' lake.

Our first day of the journey across the country was Dan's last in the hangar, finishing Jennifer's inspection.

He had mentioned that it would be important for me to get Puff ready for salt water landings, and I had read about what this means.

As we were landing, I thought We'll get ready for the salt, realized Puff could hear and expected her to flinch. Salt water operation is a terror for most seaplanes, corrosive as acid, unless care's taken.

Not a flicker of concern.

My Granma Cat landed in salt water every day.

An unfrightened remark, more than a pep talk for a difficult flight ahead.

Dan took time from his work to hand me a can of Par-Al-Ketone (which I used to call paralketone, before he taught me how important it is to pronounce chemical names correctly), thick waxy stuff one applies with a brush.

"The more work you do now," he said, "The less you'll have to do later." That sounded ominous, and the ominousity deepened when he handed me the brush and can. "You'll need to apply this, carefully, to every nut and bolt on the airplane." (Note: there are five hundred million nuts and bolts on a SeaRey.)

Three hours later, hoping never to taste Par-Al-Ketone again so long as I might live, I was ready to start fogging the interior of Puff's wings and fuselage with Corrosion-X, to protect it all, inside every strut and cranny … any place salt spray could reach, which would be everywhere.

Two hours later it was almost night, Dan finished with his inspection, I adding a vow never to breathe more than a pint of Corrosion-X for so long as I might live and by the way no more Par-Al-Ketone either thank you, ever.

I hope, dear reader, that you never have to prepare a seaplane for salt water, and wish you instead sweet dreams about bunnies hopping over lush grass and carrots.

I hoped to dream the same, a good omen for tomorrow.

CHAPTER 30

Standing By for Sunrise

The last piece fell into place today, Test Flight Day for Dan and Jennifer. If she didn't pass her flight test, Puff and I would take off for the Pacific alone.

"Do you mind if I fly alongside?" I thought it would be courteous for Puff to be in the air not far from Jennifer. Flying close, I'd be able to tell Dan which parts of his airplane were falling off during the test flight, as that would be important for him to know, and a service that Puff and I could offer.

As it turned out, however, Jennifer lost no parts to the sky. Step-taxiing first, to test her hull under stress, then airborne at low altitude, then climb to a thousand feet, then slow-flight and stalls and high speed. No parts tumbling away, Jennifer was feeling fine, thank you.

Dan kept this from being just another test flight by calling, "Wheels up for a water landing," while we were over dry land: farms and fields and trees as far as I could see.

Not wishing to say, "What?" Puff and I followed along. His airplane slowed, flaps coming down as if Jennifer was intending to land ... in that little tiny pond about the size of a tennis court! (Actually, it was about the size of a football field, which Dan felt was plenty large to teach us circling takeoffs.)

Puff and I have done circling takeoffs, but never in waters so small that they required a circling landing, as well.

If he can do it, Puff, we can.

For there he was ahead of us, touched down on what water there was in a green pasture, skimming a tight circle a few yards inside the shoreline. *Easy.*

She's changing gracefully, I thought, with experience and with a growing trust in who she is. I pretended to be so sure about me. Of course we can do this.

"Wheels up flaps down, boost pump on, power back," and down we went, our touchdown only a little complicated by Jennifer's wake, now filling the pond with waves crossing from all directions.

Soon as we touched, the far shore swiftly near, I pressed left rudder, held Puff's wings level and we slid sideways into a hard turn, our wake mixing with Jennifer's to thrash the surface into broken white spirals. We could have cut the power any time and stopped. Dan was merely showing us that we could do it, however, and as we started our second circle on the water he and Jennifer were in the air again.

Full throttle and for a breath or two I wondered if we'd lift into the air before the shore caught us, but Puff was right, it was easy—we were off the water seconds before grass went blurring below.

Low over Lake Apopka minutes later, Dan called, "Our first rescue. Wheels up for the water."

Jennifer touched down and coasted to a red dot in the water, retrieved it into the cockpit and lifted off again, all in less than a minute.

Then it was back to their home lake again, the two seaplanes touching down together, skating like summer ice-boats down the wavelets to Jennifer's ramp and hangar.

Engines stopped, Puff and Jennifer dripping water, Dan showed his rescue. It was a balloon, a red balloon with a length of wicked polyethylene attached. I couldn't be certain at the time, but as I flashed by overhead I thought a saw a young turtle, swimming blissfully unaware, directly for that entangling line. Chances are today that Dan had saved that turtle's life.

He shrugged off recognition of what he had done, as though picking killer balloons from the water was sport for him, and changed the subject.

Yet that very noon came confirmation that by their service in rescuing the turtle, Dan and Jennifer have been accepted and appointed to join the Ferret Rescue Service, Air Group One, a position for which only one other human pilot and seaplane have been chosen.

I was delighted and happy for him, though typically he put the honor and responsibility aside to consider later, in a time of quiet.

"Jennifer's flying perfectly," he said. "There's nothing left to fix."

Yet he did reach for the can of Par-Al-Ketone, and began to coat every new nut and bolt installed during Jennifer's inspection.

He worked so slowly, I was shamed that I had not followed his suggestions to do my own Par-Al-Ketone-ing with the greatest care and attention. Thus I turned back and improved what I had done:

(Before conscience attack)

(After. Could still have done better on this Bolt # 12,763,519 but did not. Moved on to Bolt #12,763,520 instead.)

Jennifer's radio did need some replacing of its antenna and took the rest of the day for the job. As my Aircraft Radio Repairperson certificate was never issued, I took an hour to go over some mental notes with my own engine shut down, which gave Dan the idea that I may have fallen asleep.

Antenna installed, we were all four of us ready to fly. South Florida now smothered in thunderstorms and forecast to remain so, we solved a difficult aviation problem as many pilots do: we changed our destination.

We'll not fly to Everglades City and the Florida Keys, as we had planned. Instead, weather permitting, we're off to Washington State tomorrow morning by way of Crystal River, the Gulf Coast, and points north by west.

That's our current mind. I wonder what will happen come sun-up.

CHAPTER 31

Best Day Flying, Ever?

H ard to say, there have been so many magnificent days in the air, but if today isn't at the top it's way high on the list.

In the air by nine a.m., early fogs turned into clear skies. Striking beautiful country that hour of the morning. Eight hours' flying today, all new experience: boy's desert island dreams, Jennifer's landing-gear failure, hours of low-level flying over untouched lands; in short, everything I was wishing for and some I wasn't, in one day.

These two spotless SeaReys, by the end of the day, would be covered in sand and salt and flights become stories they will tell to hangars-full of airplanes in years to come.

Here's Dan Nickens, first minute of first hour of first day of our transcontinental flight, unaware that what would

be an in-flight emergency to any other pilot would happen to him in less than three hours.

Jennifer follows a lost river in green-jungle Florida: Lakes bluer than the sky;

Puff's first sight of a Florida key, floating at the edge of the Gulf of Mexico:

She gazes long and silent at the sea, stretching way out beyond a horizon she would fly to cross, and thousands beyond:

Travels with *Puff*

Jennifer's experience handed free to Puff: her first ocean landing, first salt water, first uninhabited desert island. Delicious adventure!

We turned east again, across the Florida coast, as it was about time for fuel.

We were set to land at Perry Field, Puff and me in the lead, descending the last few hundred feet to the runway, when Dan called on the radio.

"Two isn't landing. Wheels won't come down."

In almost any other airplane, here's an emergency situation. "Wheels won't come down," means a gear-up sliding crash, trailing a sheet of sparks from a concrete runway. Rarely hazardous for crew and passengers, it's always damage for the airplane, unless somehow it's fixed before touchdown.

"Roger," I said, "Lead's on the go."

I look at those words in print and shake my head. Here's what I was saying to other pilots who might have been landing at the airport:

"Those two airplanes which look as if they're going to land at the airport, they're not. They're heading back up into the sky and they'll call again if they decide to try landing later on. Go ahead and land if you feel like it, they won't be using the runway or getting in your way."

Here's what I was saying, in the same words, to Dan:

"I understand you've got a problem. As the flight leader just now, I've changed my mind, too, about landing. I'm coming in with full power as I transmit these words, and climbing back up to altitude where you can see if there's a way to get Jennifer's wheels to come down for a runway landing. Puff and I will be flying alongside. We can't do a thing to help you or Jennifer, but we can move close and take a look at her landing gear and see if perhaps it's coming down fine and the problem is the landing gear indicator. If it is, we can go back and land at the airport. If it isn't, we'll go wherever you decide to go. We know that you have an hour's fuel remaining and somehow you're going to figure out what to do before Jennifer's engine stops. You will be the flight leader and Puff and I are at your service."

To which Dan didn't reply because he didn't need to. One talks, in the air, when one has something important to say. Otherwise, one does not press the microphone Transmit button. The nice thing about flying, with certain rare exceptions, is that nobody chats. As this was about to be an exception, I said, "SeaRey, go Gator." With that, we switched the radio frequency to a little-used channel where we could talk without interfering with other air traffic.

Puff and I moved close to Jennifer as we climbed. Her wheels were tucked up, she looked fine.

"Wheels coming down," said Dan. We watched, from thirty feet away. The right main wheel came down, the tailwheel and left main wheel stayed up. The problem was not with the indicator.

"Try some negative G," I said. What I meant was, "Dan, maybe there's something binding in the system, and if you made the airplane weightless, or moved the force of gravity in the opposite direction from Down, it would free the system enough to let it work properly."

Meanwhile Puff was worried, talking to Jennifer: *Are you OK? Are you frightened? What's going to happen?*

To which Jennifer replied, as best I can translate: *There's nothing they can repair in the sky, Puff. A cable's jammed, I can't get my left wheel down no matter what my pilot tries in the air.*

Not the assurance Puff was hoping for.

You can't land! If … Will you … How will you …?

Jennifer, cool and calm as morning air, I sense she smiled at her sister's concern.

No worries, Puff. Dan's going to see that it's going to take tools, and you watch—he's going leave the wheels up, find some water and land there just as if nothing's wrong, we'll taxi to the shore, he'll spend an hour and un-jam the cable. You watch. My pilot can fix anything!

She was right about that, and Dan was right too, when he said, "I don't think negative G will help. But it'll be fun and I'll try. Give me some room."

I turned Puff to slide clear, and we watched. Jennifer nosed down, sudden like a hawk, gaining speed, then soared back upwards. As she did, Dan pushed the control stick forward, and his airplane flew a lofting curve from up to down. Through the middle of that curve everything in the plane went weightless, and in that moment Dan moved the landing gear switch to DOWN. The right wheel came down. Not the left wheel, not the tailwheel.

"No luck," somebody said.

"Let's find some water," said Dan, and brought the right wheel up again. "Where's the nearest river?" I wished we were still in the lake country, with thousands of places to land, but if wishes were cinnamon rolls …

We could go back to the Gulf, I thought, though fresh water would be better, and a river's closer. I checked the map. "South a bit," I said, "about ten miles."

We turned south, and just as Jennifer had predicted, it happened.

Landed on the river, taxied to shore, Puff and I beached near Jennifer. I got out of the cockpit, walked up the riverbank to Dan.

"Something has decided that we need to have a quiet lunch today," he said.

He reached for a sandwich, I brought my bag of cookies and granola bars.

"Cable jumped off the pulley," he said. "I've never seen that happen before."

An hour of quiet repair, the clink of steel tools on a silent riverbank.

What had begun as an emergency finished its lesson: being a seaplane has advantages.

Cable secure on its pulley, we were off again. To the Cross City airport for fuel and then on our way again north and west. Mile after mile of wilderness shoreline.

Along with a mile or two of un-wilderness shoreline, too:

Jennifer over the sea—Catalina's granddaughter. See the resemblance? From a distance, can you tell them apart?

Deserted Beach Number Two: what a feeling, touching down on rippling transparent blue sunlights flashing, stepping to a sugar-sand beach, happily self-stranded for an hour, or a day, for however long we wish. A tune being hummed, here, about freedom to live our lives as we choose. A song about choices.

These places are a few miles from where some folks live, stressed in I-have-to lives. To get from there to here you need a quest, and a way to travel. This takes time and practice and love, emphasis on the latter. Obsessing about freedom helps, too.

Puff's comment about salt water:

Sticky. It stings, a little.

She widened her respect for Granma Cat, her life in the salt.

If I've learned one lesson in all my days, it's this: *The unknown, faced time and again, brings growing confidence that we can meet any challenge along our way.*

Puff and Jennifer got fresh-water showers at the Destin/Fort Walton Beach airport.

You want a fine place to land? Destin Airport, Florida, Miracle Strip Aviation, on the south end of the field. Courteous perfect service, from the fresh-water airplane wash area to fuel to courtesy car and free cookies.

CHAPTER 32

Storms and Sharks, a Tale Along Our Journey

Remember we talked how aircraft crashes don't happen by themselves, there's always a chain of events leads to the moment things come apart?

Some wild weather had roared through the Gulf of Mexico before we left Florida heading west, monster storms going up, tops at 60,000 feet with hail, a thousand lightning strikes per minute, wildfires on the NexRad display. It had not been the kind of weather through which you'd care to fly your SeaRey on the way to Seattle.

We had lucked out on our timing so far: clear skies, a few non-deadly cumulus clouds but mostly sunshine. It was forecast to continue through the morning, but not forever. Dan and I had hoped to get past the Mississippi Delta, that cauldron of tempests, before the next storms outbroke.

To do it, we needed to have our wheels off the runway by six a.m. Steps One through Five in the chain: I slept through my phone alarm ringing, misplaced my radio headset and lost some time before I remembered I had left it in the airplane, the weather guys said the storms probably wouldn't kick off till late afternoon, I didn't listen to Puff at the airport saying go-go-go, or Dan's quiet patience as I made notes about the colors of the sky … whether to call it "wine-dark" in the direction we were headed when

I so abhor alcohol and perhaps should I call it a "tannin sky" after the color of the Suwanee River when he told me where the water got its own deep hue, but would most people who had not landed on the Suwanee in a seaplane know just what that color is … minutes stretched by with my delays and after we finally started engines and taxied for takeoff there was a long wait for air traffic clearance through a restricted area before we'd be cleared to depart. Install radios in your airplane, you chuck a little of your freedom out.

One reason and another, we took off late, link building on link in the chain that leads to trouble.

After takeoff, wheels up flaps up, boost pump off engine instruments in the green (so called since the factory paints a green arc on the engine instrument dials under the normal operating range for temperatures and pressures), I took over as flight leader as Dan needed to get some photographs (next link in chain: Richard takes over as flight leader).

I watched cumulus clouds mushroom on the horizon, the weather ahead building earlier than forecast (next link).

"SeaRey Flight," I called (I know it's just Dan and me, but on the radio I call it formally, an old military flying habit), "we'll divert south for the weather, heading two three zero the barrier islands direct the Delta."

"Roger," said Dan. It was not his job, as wingman, to question my decision as flight leader, any more than I would have questioned his were he flying as leader that morning. A wingman's job is to stay in position on the lead aircraft, period. Do not speak unless spoken to, unless you notice that your leader's airplane is on fire.

My deviation for the weather took us out to sea, the sun still shining where we flew. The water was … well, it wasn't a wild sea, but I noticed that when whitecaps begin forming on the surface of the ocean the waves are a whole lot steeper and rougher and confuseder than they are on a lake.

I sensed Puff was … alert. She didn't much care for the fact that we may not survive a landing on that water if her engine failed unless her pilot used perfect timing for a perfect landing. Yet she trusted I could do that if I had to, and her engine purred along, no hint of problems.

An hour into our weather diversion, I noticed a pod of porpoises leaping slow-motion together, breaking the sea five hundred feet below us. For some reason I thought it would be prudent to climb for more altitude. I did not notice that the porpoises seemed to be swimming away from the weather.

120   Travels with *Puff*

I had planned to follow the curving line of the barrier islands, fly just off the edge of an offshore wildlife refuge, and reach the recommended altitude of 2,000 feet as we arrived. It isn't a requirement, that altitude, it's a recommendation, pilot's discretion.

By now the sunlight was giving way to shadows on the surface. Looking ahead, I felt first-hand what I had read in books by anxious mariners: is that land ahead, the islands I knew had to be there, or is that just another of the fast-multiplying cloud shadows?

We were out of sight of land. To the left, to the right, forward and back, it was all blue sea, glass-green in shallows, light and sparkling where the sun shone through, darker and more forbidding in the shadows under the weather.

Silence from Dan, of course, though I felt that he'd be as happy for the sight of land as I would be. I was sure this compass heading would bring us to the islands and confirm my navigation, but the operative word there is "confirm," and that wasn't quite forthcoming.

Are you OK, Puff? I thought.

OK. I'm doing fine. Please don't land on the water. I don't ... feel like landing.

She was watching the sea, and her respect for her Granma Catalina, already strong, grew stronger still. Cat spent her *lifetime* over seas like this!

Puff imagined searching for a five-foot yellow life raft in the roiling waters below.

So did I. Two lemmas. Lemma One: when you fly low enough to spot a raft, you can't see very far, in any direction. Lemma Two: when you fly high enough to see farther, a raft becomes a tiny object, a speck on the water.

And when you did see it, I thought, you had to land! in those seas, rescue the survivor, and then take off again!

I could not imagine crashing eighty miles per hour, full throttle, hoping to take off over waves this stark and sharp. There are stories of Catalina flying boats whose hull-rivets sheared by impact with seas like the one underneath us now. I'm told that Cat crews carried wooden pegs which they pounded into the holes of the blown rivets, to keep the water out. I'm told there were Cats and crews that left on rescue missions and never returned.

No sight of the islands, which I should have seen by now. I looked back at Dan and Jennifer, the man and his airplane in the position a wingman should be. Aviation tradition says that when a flight leader makes some vast mistake and flies into the terrain, so faithful is a good wingman that there is not one but two holes in the mountainside.

Dan and Jennifer and Puff, they were trusting me, and ahead the clouds were lowering. Of course we could lower, too, to stay beneath the weather, but that would bring us closer to the water, reduce our visibility ahead.

I leaned forward in the seat, as though leaning would help me see. Grey sea, whitecaps, the wind increasing, quartering from behind. At least we had a tailwind, I thought, so we're moving faster than normally we would.

There ahead! The faintest line of white? Or was it the last shaft of sunlight through a hole in the clouds? Minutes passed. Surf. The white line was waves crashing on sand … the islands!

I felt a surge of relief. We were not lost at sea. In fact, we were precisely on course. The clouds were lowering, but so what?

I glanced behind, over the snow-and-sky colors of Jennifer's bright wings. The weather was closing down behind us, too. Not that turning back had been my plan, as our tailwind would become headwind if I did, slowing us down over that seething blue country going grey as I watched.

There was good news and there was bad news. The good news was that I knew exactly where we were. The bad news was that because of my delays, the weather that wasn't here two hours ago was here now, the ceiling pushing us lower.

Wildlife refuge, I thought. Recommended altitude two thousand feet. I didn't see any wildlife on the sands ahead. Had it deserted the land, fleeing a storm it knew was coming?

Recommended is not required, I thought. The pilot is responsible for the safety of his aircraft, the flight leader is responsible for the safety of every aircraft in his flight. Dan and Jennifer were trusting their lives to my judgment.

Down we came, hugging the edge of this strangely deserted refuge. Did the wildlife decide this was their sanctuary, or did some human being in the Office of Aerial Survey and Charting make that decision?

At this point I had other concerns than OASC Wildlife Fencing criteria, shafts of rain slanting now off our right wing. The only way through was straight ahead, trusting that the weather wouldn't turn to fog and force us to the sea.

The sand down there was wild with surf on the windward side of the islands, level and smooth on the lee side. At least we could land safely now, if we had to, land and ride out the storm.

That will not be my first choice, I thought.

Puff's wings flexed in the gusts.

I go where you go.

Chains of decisions, which lead to consequences. They're not just for flyers. Everyone makes decision-chains, choosing as best we can. Sometimes we survive to safe harbor, sometimes we don't.

The clouds forced us lower, by now we were a few hundred feet over the waves. I looked ahead, next sight might be sunshine on the west side of the storm. Or not.

As I was reflecting that this would not be my favorite place to have an engine failure and forced landing, my perfect silent wingman spoke.

"Sharks."

I had been looking forward, not down. Soon as I shifted my gaze, there they were, teeming in the bottle-green water below, long grey forms, sinuous, outlined against the golden floor of the sea.

Seaweed, I thought. Those forms are not sharks they are seaweed, or kelp; ocean plants take all shapes. Yet all at once the prospect of a forced landing here slipped lower on my scale of desirable events.

Besides, aren't shar—deep-water creatures? What would they be doing in shallow water?

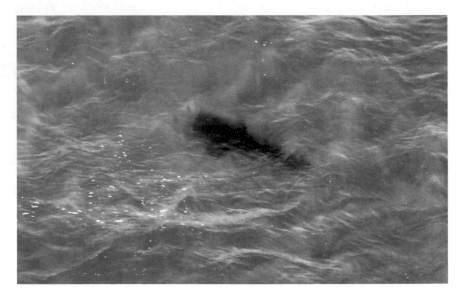

Feeding?

"Roger on the sharks," I replied.

At last it came clear. This place is not a Wildlife Refuge for Birds and Land Animals, as I had foolishly assumed, it is a Wildlife Refuge for Sharks!

If you've ever had a moment when you wondered, What am I doing here? you know how I was feeling that moment.

"Stay with me, Puff," I said aloud.

I'm with you.

I thought of Granma Cat. Is she with us too, Puff?

The island blurred below, fell behind. We flew now over shoals, crashing-grounds for waves, surfing themselves into curling flying billows of spray.

Do not think about surf. Do not think about billows or spray or sharks or engine failures. Think fly! Think go like a Cat, bore right straight on through to the Delta and the sunlight west. Heading is now two seven zero, I thought. Doesn't make any difference, I added, that me and Puff and Dan and Jennifer, we're a hundred feet over the sea. If we were a thousand feet it'd make no difference—engine trouble and we're in a cauldron with the sharks.

Out of the gray ahead, a massive structure. Land, please?

No luck, but close. An oil drilling platform. All derrick and steel lattice, a level square at the top: helicopter landing pad.

"Puff, I know it's small, but could you land on that helicopter pad, if you had to?"

Silence for a minute.

Strong wind? No gusts? Yes.

"I mean now, Puff, a twenty-mile wind, gusting twenty-eight."

She answered right away:

No.

Another platform, and another. We were a barely ten miles from land. Sharks never come that close to the mainland, do they?

Puff did not answer, as shark choices are not her area of expertise.

I decided of course they don't, that sharks definitely do not come that close to the mainland, and we were, we had to be too close to land …

A sudden line, bright green and sunlight, on the horizon, a slice of blue above.

At this point it occurred that I might begin breathing once more, and I found some pleasure in that luxury, breathing yet again as the water changed below from dark blue-grey to the color of mud. The Mississippi.

"It's dust from a million mountains," Dan would tell me later, "carried down to the delta. There are tens of thousands of feet of mud beneath that shore."

I thought it would be nice to talk with my geologist wingman now, as the Mississippi turned from sea to river, bounded by vast tracts of reeds gone emerald in oh! so welcome sunlight.

We landed at last, a four-hour flight, two SeaReys two pilots safely down at the airport in Patterson, Louisiana. And once again we had fine caring service from the folks on the ground at Perry's Flying Service: fuel and parking, cold bottled water for free and offers to help in any way.

We had planned to fly on, but Jennifer wanted to stay. She proved that, as we were taxiing for takeoff, when no warning, her engine stopped. Stopped cold and would not start again, she coasting quietly onto the grass by the taxiway.

Dan was puzzled, till he removed a carburetor float bowl. One float had inexplicably stopped floating, it had sunk in its gasoline, poured so much fuel into the engine that it stopped running. A new float kit for the carburetor takes a day by fast express.

Had Jennifer's engine stopped two hours earlier, in the rough sea and the sharks, it would have been inconvenient for us all. Had Jennifer been forced to land, Puff would have landed alongside, no matter the seas or that her engine was running fine … we would have been in trouble together.

If I've learned one lesson in all my days, it's this: *Following what we most love leads us through tests and challenges, yet something watches over us, something guides and protects along the way.*

All save the sharks now thanked her for arranging her engine failure now on the taxiway, and not then over the sea.

CHAPTER 33

Quiet Day in Louisiana

*I*t's the Corps of Engineers against the combined Red and Mississippi rivers," Dan said. "The Corps is holding its own, right now, but sooner or later in the next thousand years there's going to be a wall of water forty feet high coming down the Atchafalaya River, and the place we're standing is going to be the bottom of the new Mississippi."

Naturally I didn't believe a word, silly geology-talk. Geology major, he was, math minor, law degree, combined master's with geology and coastal and oceanographic engineering. Rock-hounds, what do you expect? Idly curious, however, I checked the Internet.

We had decided to stay one more day at the hotel in Morgan City, and all of a sudden I wished we hadn't, don't care how tired, how bad the weather this afternoon, don't care tornadoes on course, let's get Jennifer's engine running and we're outta here! A wall of water forty feet high?

Dan calmed me down. "This is not likely to happen before we leave tomorrow," he said. I stepped from the hotel-room desk back to the floor. After all, I reasoned, Dan is staying tonight at this very hotel, himself.

So I got to write in the middle of the day. Dan picked up the carburetor floats, installed them. Jennifer's engine is now running perfectly. Trouble is, can I sleep tonight, thinking of what happens with the diverting of "the

129

combined flow of the Mississippi and Red Rivers to the Atchafalaya River, which will lead to flooding along its banks in places like Morgan City, Louisiana." More than ten feet deep flooding, after that first 40 feet has whistled through.

Not likely to happen before tomorrow. Just in case, though, I'll add 30 feet to Puff's tiedown ropes and ask for a room four floors up.

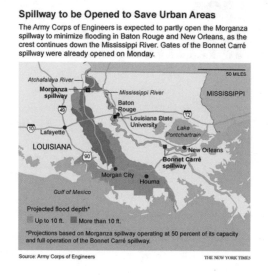

Spillway to be Opened to Save Urban Areas

The Army Corps of Engineers is expected to partly open the Morganza spillway to minimize flooding in Baton Rouge and New Orleans, as the crest continues down the Mississippi River. Gates of the Bonnet Carré spillway were already opened on Monday.

Projected flood depth*

Up to 10 ft.   More than 10 ft.

*Projections based on Morganza spillway operating at 50 percent of its capacity and full operation of the Bonnet Carré spillway.

Source: Army Corps of Engineers   THE NEW YORK TIMES

I'm glad Dan's other degree isn't nuclear engineering.

CHAPTER 34

Major Cool Day

Sometimes days that begin a little scary turn out to be worth the courage it takes to live them anyway. From the picture below, guess which direction we needed to fly:

If you picked the lowest greyest most dismal part of the horizon for the heading we wanted, you win the prize of how it feels when you say, "Let's take off and see what it looks like when we get there."

It turned out that its dark was worse than its bite, but it was some comfort to me along the way, knowing that Dan was leader so if anything bad happened it would happen to him first.

Soon as we were in the air, wheels retracted as the last of the runway flashed below, it began to rain. My job was to say nothing about that, but to fly our position close to Jennifer's left wing.

It occurred to me, as we flew, that I had no idea what day it was today. I thought about that for the longest time as we slipped lower under the clouds … try as I might, I couldn't remember. It had been so long since what-day-is-it mattered that it was a funny bemusement, flying: could this be a Monday? No. Monday was a couple weeks ago. So it must be Friday. No. Is it Tuesday, then?

Later I found that we had flown through one of those places where the days have no names, they're just "Day."

The rain was a half-hearted warning, from weather that didn't much care whether we flew or not, so we did and it fell behind us. Ahead opened the Atchafalaya River, which was to become the Mississippi which was to become the Red, our Interstate freeway till it ran out of water, way up northwest from us.

An hour after takeoff, Dan called, "Wheels up for a water landing," Jennifer (feeling frisky now with her carburetor fixed) banked up on one wing and rode down an air-slide to the river. Happy with that idea, and with warm sunshine breaking through all around us, Puff turned to follow.

Every landing in the wilderness, one checks for hazards on the surface, floating logs, tree branches, anything that breaks the surface of the water. Sometimes there lurk hazards out of sight: underwater rocks and snags, but such it is flying seaplanes as in living every day—it's a calculated risk to get out of bed, but we do it anyway.

Our first risk of the day (or thousandth, if you count the details) paid off:

Calm we found, of the sort one finds in remote places, far from electricity and all that dances on its spiky fingers. Quiet from no speakers no traffic no sirens no radio no television no nothing but sky, and slow gentle riverside. One doesn't know how much we take background noise for granted till it's gone.

I sat for a while in the cockpit, Puff's bow resting on the sand. I was perfectly comfortable, infinitely happy for all the difficult times glad times, decisions go stop left right up down that had brought me here this nameless day.

Puff asleep, I thanked her anyway. What a brave little thing she is, doing her best where she's never gone before, trusting me in spite of my flaws and errors to keep us alive.

"Lunchtime." Dan brought an apple from his airplane, I brought my bag of cookies and a thing of water, hiked up the sand and settled still for a while. Not much talking, a whole lot of gratitude that such lovely places and times stretch around us, embrace us whether or not we embrace them back.

"This is not so bad," he said, after a while.

I didn't know whether to nod yes this is not so bad or to shake my head no this is not so bad at all. There's no understatement I know, says how lovely is our freedom to live as we choose.

That's why we had come, this the point of our gentle adventure with the two little airplanes—to find if we could somehow jump the tracks of our daily lives, fly off and discover the planet we've spread around us for so long as we choose to stay.

We came not to travel to one place, but to discover there are an indefinite number of them, sanctuaries, physical and not, a three-dimension sea of them within the reach of a changed mind.

I thought about that, through five slow cookies or more: here's what it means to be free: we can do what we wish with our lives and our skills, if we choose to do … we're not required to live for others.

Then without a word Dan and I knew it was time to be on our way, destination unknown save for more like this warm-sand riverbank.

I thought, as does most every visitor to this vast silent stream, that before me spread the same views that rolled past the eyes of Samuel Clemens, a century deep in Ago. How Mark Twain's ideas and his smile have changed my world! His life on the Mississippi, I thought, melting into Dan's

and mine while that dark water flows, its odd sands, which begin to swallow folks who stand in the moving shallows. (They only swallow folks a little past their ankles, but it's a strange feeling, as the sinking begins.)

How easy it would be, to come to this sandbar, and stay for a day or two, then off to the next and stay a day or two there, then off to the next ...

I was to learn, a boy reading adventure stories, that "desert island" doesn't mean the Sahara surrounded by water, it means "deserted island," trees and springs and grassland, sand and earth and ponds untouched by anyone in all the world. How I had yearned to find such a place, now they were all around me.

Be patient, child, hold it in your thought.

Hours next, we left the Mississippi and flew the Red River, mile after mile of it sweeping beneath us.

It's become a familiar call: "Wheels up for the water." Yet no sandbar below, what can Dan be looking for?

In the air again, knowing I was wondering, he pressed the microphone button: "Wanted to see the flowers."

Flowers there are many, in our wild places. And trees:

I felt as innocent as Puff-in-a-human-body, for all my having flown high and fast, now seeing this country become vaster intimate here-and-now, thanks to Puff-in-wings. How important they are, human and otherwise, the friends we choose to open our doors and windows!

Hugging the river, I turned to watch Jennifer and Dan flying alongside. Ten feet beneath them, in the other dimensions of the mystical rivers below, flew two parallel Jennifer/Dans ... shadow and reflection of the ones in our world. How many other usses, I thought, in how many dimensions, brush us this minute, shimmering mirrors, some unaware of our existence, others caring about our choices as we care about theirs?

Godspeed, alternate selves, I thought, I wish you adventure and discovery and the sweep of love through all your lives!

Later I found that Dan was seeing the same, thinking the same before me:

How many otherworld friends and powers, I wondered, fly with us every day, unseen?

"We're about at the end of the navigable river," Dan called. "It gets shallow ahead."

Before it did, though, a major sandbar, and you guessed it: "Wheels up for a water landing." That call is so important, the determination not to crash wheels-down in the water, that seaplane pilots never tire of saying it aloud.

Here's what we found this time:

Travels with _Puff_

Each place different from the other, world subtly shifted, yet that same calm peace, soaking into the visitor.

"You know what, Dan, the sand's firm. We could have landed wheels-down here!"

The idea struck us at the same instant: one plane on land, one in the river. "I'll do it," he said.

Then he was off the water and gone to the sky. What an odd feeling, left alone, watching Jennifer fly away!

She'll be back, Puff. She's just going to do a little trick for us.

The silhouette in the air turned toward us, down to the river, but its wheels remained up, Dan inspecting the sand runway from the air. Wisdom to do so ... strike that buried branch on landing, the one at the far right of the photo, and he'd be visiting longer than he planned.

Now she knew what to avoid, Jennifer climbed again, turned into the wind, and this time her wheels came down, she floated to touch on the sand.

So, sure enough, we had in one frame both worlds of the amphibian airplane:

We let that sink through us for a time, changing our knowledge of the possible, and then the next challenge touched us both. "If we take off side by side, Richard, Jennifer on the land and Puff on the water, who'll be in the air first?"

Conventional wisdom says the landplane flies off quicker than the seaplane, since there's less drag to overcome. Our twin aircraft, we'd soon find out.

Jennifer taxied to the end of the sand, Puff taxied up-river past the sandbar, turned and headed parallel to her sister. Soon as we were side by side, both throttles went to takeoff power, spray flying beneath Puff, sand behind Jennifer.

Conventional wisdom was so, but not by much. Three seconds after Jennifer's wheels were in the air, Puff was flying, too, the last drops of river turning to vapor in her trail.

We turned back on course as the sun lowered. I was dimly aware how much I was melting to become Puff, and she to become me. I no longer needed the tachometer, for instance, to know her engine speed, down to the finest measure. Engine revolutions of 4800 rpm sound different ... the hum of the propeller subtly lower than the hum of 4850 rpm, or of 4825. I stopped checking the engine tachometer that afternoon and listened instead to my own new heartbeat.

If I've learned one lesson in all my days, it's this: *Plan our way with trust in a positive guiding spirit, we find more gifts along our path than ever we expect.*

Dan pressed his microphone button. "Texarkana tonight?"

"You're leader," I replied.

Texarkana it was.

This may be the way, I thought—not seaplanes but shared fears and joys and quality of adventure, which helps people round the world change toward each other from caution to trust.

Travels with *Puff*

Chapter 35

Fears, and Flying Anyway

There's another FLASH! of lightning in the dark outside the hotel in Stephenville, Texas. The computer's showing storm cells the color of lit matches flaring, right on us.

There was no room in the hangars here for Puff and Jennifer after our flight from Texarkana today. They're double-tied down, control locks and covers on but just now in the midst of this weather (FLASH! again and the sound of dynamite rattling the window) … just now in the midst of the storm I'm practicing relaxing, relaxing (FLASH! at least it's not in the direction of the airport), that nothing can touch the truth of Puff's being or mine or Dan's or Jennifer's. The truth of us, the spirit, is not subject to storms of earth or whims of belief in material worlds.

Puff was frightened before Dan and I left the airport this evening. Her only other thunderstorm, she was safe in the hangar at Fantasy of Flight, with the gang at the Aero Club. Now she's outside, the winds gusting to 38 knots, about 44 mph. They're from the north, just about on her nose. Winds of that speed, if it weren't for her tiedowns, she'd fly without her pilot, go tumbled to death.

The forecast calls for winds to 52 mph from the south, and hail. Forecast's a guess and it's most often wrong. The only event not forecast tonight is tornadoes. We took our chances with these when we decided to fly this journey, as earlier voyagers took their chances with whirlpools and sea-serpents.

So I'll know this again for her as well as for myself: she and I and all, we're perfect expressions of perfect life, we can neither be harmed nor destroyed, no matter beliefs or appearances. We're here to share the gifts of our discovery and our lives with those somewhere somewhen who may care for what we find along our way.

Nothing in the worlds of illusion can touch or change the truth of our being. We are guided and protected in our dreams by the fact that we're dreaming, we are led along our flickering path by our highest self, in whatever form it may decide to take. That form may even be the appearance of storm, a chance for us to test the trust we have in our own knowing. A test which I intend to pass and take Puff along with me, no matter what.

At one time I wouldn't have believed the intensity of my connection with the spirit of this little seaplane. I suppose I could explain it, but I maybe I can't … just now I'm not into explaining what so moves and touches me.

It's ten minutes later. Radar shows the worst of the storm has moved over us. I have the feeling that Puff and Jennifer (whom Puff has taken to calling "Little Cat" in respect for her flying experience) are wet and shaken but undamaged. Puff may have lost her engine cover to the wind. I sense there was no hail.

Thanks to my writing habit, we were late to take off this morning from Texarkana. Dan was leader for the departure, I'm happy to say, and I left there grateful to be on our way. It's a big place, corporate jets, control tower. That used to be my world (not the corporate jets, but control towers and approach controls and instrument flight plans and boring through clouds—it's called flying "in the system"), it is not my world today.

Puff has a radio and a radar transponder as they are required if one wishes to fly in certain areas of the country, but they are not natural to her and secretly I'd like to pull them out to save the weight. Heart and spirit, she's an off-road airplane, what pilots call a stick-and-rudder aircraft, as she's proven in the weeks we've flown together. As I seem to have become a stick-and-rudder pilot, it's no wonder we get along.

I was a disaster after I took over as leader this morning. My wingman had to remind me that I was about to fly into controlled airspace, something that should have horrified me but didn't, my guess being in that particular airspace nobody would have noticed or cared.

One after another, I found three lakes in which I hoped to land, every one of them prickled through with dead trees and stumps and logs. When they make a new lake by damming rivers in Texas, they don't much care that it looks like a pincushion when they're finished, even boats having to pick their way through the forests of dead trees towering through the surface. The water looked cool, but it might as well have been mirage-water, for all those underwater stumps to blast and sink a careless seaplane.

It was hard flying, through a hot day. No river below for safe landing, I flew a thousand feet and higher above the ground, giving us gliding room to an open space if an engine stopped. At that altitude thermals were everywhere, confused and broken by the wind, the air rough as melting icebergs. Some days, flying and living, one chooses to shut up and slam through whatever mass of turbulence comes our way. After two and a half hours of this, I was glad to land for fuel.

Next leg, just before we got pounded to death, Dan found a river right out of the Hole-in-the Wall from *Butch Cassidy and the Sundance Kid*. Never was I so glad to hear him call "Wheels up for the water."

Puff and I landed a hundred yards downstream from Jennifer. "I'm going to explore this cove," said Dan. When we turned to follow him, he and she had disappeared.

We chased down along the bank and found the entrance, two wingspans wide, into a hidden water-garden.

After the heat and wind and rocks in the air, thunderstorms diverting our course left and right, this was paradise.

Dipping my hands into cool water as we taxied slowly in that beautiful place, after that I allowed as how I was ready for more pounding.

Jennifer slipped out the hidden doorway, and Puff followed.

Back in the air, thudding and bashing toward Abilene, Dan called with welcome news: "Abilene's got thunderstorms. We'll land Stephenville." It would make only four and a half hours' flying today, but that was fine with me.

The sky solid misty grey to the north as we turned to land, thunderstorms embedded there.

Finally on the ground, we double-tied and covered the airplanes, made

them ready as best we could for what might come in the night.

If I've learned one lesson in all my days, it's this: *You do your best, and you call down your angels, and somehow they see you through your storms.*

CHAPTER 36

Morning Comes

The thunderstorms from the lightning night were gone by sunrise. Early to the airport, Dan and I found Puff and Jennifer barely jostled at their tiedowns, undamaged.

Were my fears for the little seaplane silly, or did my affirmations make a difference? I guess they made a difference to me, and that's what matters when I'm facing destructions.

The concern, I thought, wasn't foolish, at least for a mortal, as storm-winds sometimes break things. Our little seaplanes survived the night, and though Puff's engine cover was shredded it was not blown to North Dakota by the thunders. I breathed a happy sigh, untied the multi-lines that held Puff through the night, and spun her round to face the morning's breeze while I ran her preflight inspection.

I set the altimeter, reminded that the ground elevation is rising as we fly west. A few days ago, flying at 1,200 feet above sea level kept us well clear of the ground. Now 1,200 feet above sea level is scraping the treetops ... the land under our way ahead will rise to 7,000 feet above sea level, and higher.

North and west stretches the difficult part of our adventure: high ground, high temperature, and rock, so far as one can see.

Sometimes it's simple, sometimes it's hard going, yet the time always comes, doesn't it, when we leave our tiedowns and get back to flying?

In half an hour we were airborne again, thudding through the winds. Above a highway for a few miles, I watched while the cars below moved from behind us on the road, passed us and disappeared ahead. Later the wind increased.

The world of aviation, I realized, is divided into two parts: the faster machines, and Those Who Get Passed by Cars. It is the latter group, I think, who watch with most gratitude when the tables turn, feel the reckless joy of actually passing over a Volkswagen on the open road!

Before long, though, highways were behind us, and the land below looked not quite so welcoming to us as moonscapes to a passing astronaut. Not quite, since the moon lacks clumps of mesquite every twelve feet in any direction. Dan and Jennifer flew blissfully, enjoying landforms down low, cautious me kept Puff high, in case her engine failed we'd have time to pick the openest spot to land.

Not two days ago there was water everywhere, there was no place we couldn't land. All of a sudden, water's scarce:

Are you worried, my pilot? Puff asked this, full of confidence. *I've got wheels!*

It was hard to explain my wisdom to her, flying up at airline altitudes while Dan and his plane flew carefree over the mesquite. What difference does it make, I thought. If Jennifer has an engine failure, Puff and I will be landing in the brush alongside, anyway.

Nevertheless, everyone flies at the altitude that's comfortable for them, and higher, today, was mine. And besides, in loose cross-country formation there's nothing says a wingman has to be tucked in tight to the leader. Unless Dan asked me to close it up, he agreed that loose and high was fine with him. Even high, it was hard to imagine landing spots.

Travels with *Puff*

That's the profile we took, today, Bold and Cautious flying together. That's not so rare, I thought. We choose partners to fly with who bring us balance.

It was easy at the time, we hovered above like Dan's otherworld angel, yet when I snapped some photos, they turned into Find the Jennifer challenges:

Yes, she is in this photograph. You will need your magnifying glass:

This one's easier (and more comfortable when the engine stops):

Either a SeaRey is an awfully small airplane, or we live on an awfully large planet.

Puff insists that she is not so awfully small, so there you have it.

What was that a while ago about flight plans, instrument flight plans? Don't little airplanes on nice days need to file a flight plan, in order to be safe? It's a pilot's grudge, in any story of a light aircraft accident: "... the pilot had not filed a flight plan."

Sounds as if the pilot and his airplane were just floating around the sky, doesn't it, unwatched by someone responsible like Air Traffic Control? Stuff and nonsense! The only purpose a flight plan serves for good-weather flying is that it gives search and rescue teams some idea of where to look for a missing aircraft. No other reason. Nobody's watching, nobody's caring, nor should they be.

Not once did Dan or I file a flight plan don't you want to know why. Because we're our own search and rescue. We do not want anyone searching for us after we've changed our minds about our destination and decided to stay overnight on some riverbank uninterrupted by rotor blades and search-lights. If we need help we'll ask if it's available. If we don't or it isn't, we'll take care of ourselves thank you. Want to get an airplane pilot to muttering? Tell her how dangerous are all those little airplanes, aloft without flight plans!

Fuel, we couldn't say it was running low, but we turned and slogged through the turbulence to the Floydada airport just in case, as we are each of us cautious about low-fuel flying. What would we do, nearly out of gas, if the airport we depended on for fuel had something happen I don't know what, and it was closed? Though such a thing might happen once in practically never, the thoughtful pilot keeps the possibility in mind.

"Wheels down for landing," called Dan as Jennifer turned to her down-wind leg in the landing pattern. The wind was across the runway, and at least 20 mph, at that. I planned to angle Puff's landing roll ten degrees or so across the runway, into the wind.

"Whisky Tango's turning base to final," he called. Puff and I began our turn, to land behind him.

Jennifer didn't land. She pulled up, flew off to one side of the landing strip.

"Two," he called, "they're paving the runway."

Sure enough, the strip was liquid black tar, hot in the Texas afternoon. Jennifer circled, raised her wheels, and about that time a stranger's voice on the radio:

"Floydada airport's closed. Aircraft circling Floydada airport, the runway's closed."

"Roger," Dan replied.

The voice was all Texas: "Sorry, boys."

"No worries," said Dan.

No worries? Sure enough, Dan, when once-in-never happens: the airport's closed, no worries because you didn't wait to land till we were nearly out of fuel.

"SeaRey Two," he called, "we'll fly to Plainview. Twenty-five miles ahead."

All I had to do was to press the microphone button and say, "Roger." When it comes to making decisions, being a wingman is not a difficult job.

Dan raised the Plainview airport on the local radio frequency (called "Unicom," for your information since you'll be learning to fly soon).

"Plainview wind is two four zero at seventeen gusting twenty-nine."

Twenty-nine knots is 33 miles per hour, and it was twenty degrees cross to runway 22. Now that sounds super-technical, doesn't it? But we've flown together long enough, you and us, that you remember that runways are numbered for the compass direction they face. Runway 22 is laid out on the magnetic heading of 220 degrees. So the wind, coming from 240 degrees, is blowing 20 degrees across the runway, from the right side.

By now, Puff and I laugh at crosswinds. (When we're together in the air, we laugh at them. When the winds are thunderstorms and we're on the ground there's no laughing.)

Dan and Jennifer may or may not have been merry, but they looked that way, touched down pretty as a picture, angled into the wind. Puff and I did the same.

She says it more than I do, now: *Piece of cake.*

"You be careful, Puff," I said. "Overconfidence is dangerous, flying."

Schmoverconfidence!

She was laughing at me, but I knew I'd best fly careful, now, for the both of us.

We taxied for fuel, and Dan found there was a hangar available for the night! A big hangar, and welcome, in this wind.

Airplanes safe, us driving to the hotel, I asked. "What were you and Jennifer doing so low, Dan? If her engine failed, you'd … We were up high, even so I didn't see any place to land. It's all brush and rocks!"

He looked at me, surprised. "Are you kidding? There were all kinds of places to land! This wind, our landing roll is only going to be a few feet. I almost landed a couple of times, to show you. But they weren't the prettiest places, for pictures."

I had to admit there was likely a truth in what he said. When a SeaRey lands at 35 mph, and the wind is 25 mph, then her wheels are touching the ground at around 10 mph. Not a deadly scenario, and one can land in a tiny space, at that speed.

Dan returned to the airport this afternoon, troubleshooting Jennifer's reluctant carburetor, which now wants to be venting fuel overboard. Her engine is running fine, but that engine is wasting fuel and the problem needs to be solved before we take on the Continental Divide.

Back at the hotel, over dinner: "Am I glad we have that hangar tonight!"

Uh-oh, I thought. "Dan, why are you glad we have that hangar tonight?"

"The wind! I was working on the engine in the hangar and sure, it was windy outside, but all of a sudden it sounded like a freight train, the way they say tornadoes sound going by. I have never heard a gust of wind like that … it shook that whole big hangar!"

Thank you thank you guardian angels, I thought. Thank you Granma Cat! Safe at night through the thunderstorm in Stephenville, today comes the one time this trip a tornado-like event passes by, the Little Cats are snuggled in their hangar!

It's thoughtful on our journeys, I think, to acknowledge those angels who take a minute to shield us with their wings. If I were an angel, I'd appreciate that.

If I've learned one lesson in all my days, it's this: *The more we believe there's invisible positive guidance in our lives, the more it's true for us, and the more it works every day.*

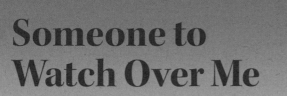

CHAPTER 37

Someone to Watch Over Me

To the hangar this morning, wind howling, shuddering and banging the tin sides of the building, guess what rested gently on the floor, inches from Puff's nose:

A feather, for me, is a multi-level reminder that what we imagine comes true for us, that there's more to our world and the way it works than we see with our eyes, that delicate powers guide us along the paths we choose to follow.

Of course the feather resting near Puff was a coincidence. Birds come sometimes to build nests in hangar-roof trusses. Even so, there was no other feather in the hangar and I had to remember hard to think of when I had seen a feather by my airplane, in the past, ever.

This was the day that Dan and I had agreed: we are going to play this mountain crossing carefully. If Jennifer's carburetor isn't working right, if the wind keeps shrieking at us thirty miles per hour, if one or both of us are intuitionally challenged by the prospect of facing large mountains with small airplanes, today shall be spent in Resting and Regrouping. We have all three conditions right now: No-go, No-go, No-go. Rest and Regroup it is.

Dan had been up earlier for a flight test on the carburetor, came back to the hotel with news that weather stations to the north and west are clocking winds over 50 mph. These are not forecast but measured winds, careening over West Texas right now.

It may be somewhere in my journal, before ever we left Florida, I was thinking to allow a couple days to our voyage "in case we get pinned down in Texas by winds." Not uncommon for light aircraft, yet that intuition was spot on. Or it could be that holding it in thought made it come true?

His flight test went eerily well, Dan said. He measured Jennifer's engine fuel flow at 4.9 gallons per hour at 5,000 revolutions per minute: exactly the figure she was designed to use. And yet there's still fuel venting into her propeller, and that's not right.

"I'll call the engine expert tomorrow," he said. "I'll ask what he'd do."

We agreed that this was no day for travel, but a fine one to work on the airplanes, take care of minor issues, get them cleaned of the dust and spray of travel.

I got to counting, as I tinkered with Puff, refastening her airspeed pitot tube, removing a useless exhaust stack from the muffler, rubbing her surfaces down with fresh water—I got to counting the number of coincidences that led to our resting safe inside, today, while the windstorm shrieked outside.

In that instant a new fist of wind huffed and hammered the sheet-metal roof, reminding how glad I am that I'm not a three little pig, that the plan to build this hangar from straw was not approved and the decision to make it out of steel was.

I counted. Were it not for the fact that Floydada airport runway happened to be slathered with hot tar yesterday, I thought, the single day that airport has been closed in let me guess twenty years, Dan and I would have landed there, fueled and flown past Plainview, Texas.

We would have flown by this airport, with this hangar which happened to be open and empty enough for two SeaReys with room to spare when every other airport we've landed at had zero hangar-space available.

We happened to find this refuge shortly before the mother of all dust devils passed directly over Puff and Jennifer with the sound and thunder of a freight-train tornado but not the explode-your-hangar power to wreck the planes as they surely would have been wrecked had they been tied down outside.

Because we stopped here, Dan was able to repair Jennifer's carburetor to the point where it meets factory specifications, if not yet to settle his mind about the fuel venting.

Because we stopped here, I learned what I hadn't known before, that Puff's coolant level should properly be half-filling the radiator overflow reservoir instead of leaving it empty. Had we not leisurely have been inspecting the airplanes, Puff would have departed into a 95-degree sky toward the mountains with a radiator near empty of coolant. I would not have bought the 50/50 coolant mix, available in town, to refill the radiator and an extra container to spare.

Had we not stopped here, Dan would not have found the material to repair the slow leak in Jennifer's right main tire.

Since we stopped here he took time to replace Jennifer's rudder-lock blown away by the night-riding thunderstorm in Stephenville.

Had we not made our careful inspections, I would not have found my lost sunglasses fallen between the seats to the bottom of the hull.

Dan would not have decided to leave to this airport a number of heavy items, keeping Jennifer as light as possible for the flying ahead.

It occurred to me, pounding through the jarring flaming air yesterday, that our shakedown flights are over. We're not practicing for this journey any more, we're flying it. Plainview, Texas is one of the few places in several hundred miles where we could have rested and regrouped as we have. It may yet happen, but I'll not be surprised if we can't find hangar-space for the airplanes in the next 1800 miles flying. (Note from the future: Correct. Puff and Jennifer didn't see the inside of a hangar for the rest of the journey.)

Had it not been for a tar-soaked runway over the horizon south, and the cascade of positive consequences that followed, I would not have found a feather, this morning, by my airplane.

CHAPTER 38

Decisions

We had a long discussion, Dan and I, filled with pros and cons, consider this'es and on-the-other-hands. Our final conclusion: there is almost nothing on this trip that is worth dying for, or wrecking a faithful trusting airplane.

No schedule is worth dying for, nor need to fly any particular route, nor distress at staying longer than we planned somewhere along our way. No photograph's worth getting killed, although I sense Dan is unconvinced on that one.

We've agreed that from here on, if one of us goes down in difficult terrain, and exits his airplane in a clearly chipper condition, the other will fly to the nearest airport and commence a ground or helicopter rescue effort.

If the one on the ground is not so chipper after landing, or doesn't get out of the cockpit, the other will land nearby regardless of terrain, and render assistance.

Note after this conversation: My intuition tells me Dan's going to take Jennifer down low over impossible rocks, when he fancies a good photo to be got. If her engine fails in one or another of those places, Puff and I become the Dan & Jennifer Rescue Team. The reverse is not the case, as Puff and I will never get into trouble.

I feel like Mr. Phelps of the Impossible Missions Force: "If you choose to accept this mission ..." and the cassette tape has turned to smoke. Except we've chosen to accept the mission in advance, no matter how impossible. Times like these, I realize there is some wisdom, staying in bed all day every day.

Having made this decision, of course it needs be tested. Dan was on the phone early, ordering a new carburetor for Jennifer, express delivered to his hotel room. The engine guru in Florida agrees: it's wrong for a carburetor to vent fuel overboard even though it's perfect in all other respects.

This will give us a day or two in Plainview, and in that time we might as well replace Jennifer's tailwheel assembly, as well.

Puff had mentioned some time ago that all things being equal she would feel better with a new tailwheel retraction cable, her present cable serviceable but frayed.

Dan has inspected the cable, taking great care. One or two tiny strands are broken. "There's nothing wrong with this cable. She'll go a long time yet before it begins to be a problem."

(Puff values and respects Dan and his experience. She would feel better with a new cable, please, at such time as it may be convenient.)

None of these repairs are critical. We could likely fly the remaining half of the country with no maintenance whatever. We choose not to do that, for the spirit murmuring What If: If the carburetor fails over some rocky canyon, would you wish you had fixed it when you could have: Yes or No?

Thus our talk about what's worth dying (or being stranded with a pile of airplane wreckage in the mountains on a bark and pine-needle diet in bear country for a week or so) for.

To the airport on a sudden-cold morning, I pulled the hooded sweat-shirt from my survival pack, and switched from water-shoes to boots.

I filled Puff's radiator and reservoir, cleaned up the antifreeze splashed all over the engine while doing so, found my spare Swiss Air Officer's Escape and Evasion Attack and Destroy knife and presented it to Dan so that he will cease constantly asking for mine in the course of each day's minor mechanical needs.

Not long after the presentation (for which I suspect he was more pleased than he dared show), he made a correction: "Thank you for my Swiss Air Officer's Escape and Evasion Rescue and Restore knife. Unless you think Attack and Destroy may be on our agenda?"

I allowed as how I did not plan on attacking and destroying anyone, ever, at least not with the tools on this knife.

With naught we could more do with the aircraft, Dan noticed a strange sight across the runway, and we drove to investigate.

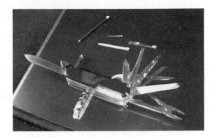

Here's what he spotted, up close—tiptanks missing, canopy gone opaque, engine intakes sealed, but there she was, the Lockheed T-33A, the first jet aircraft I'd ever flown.

The T-33 and I both concede we may look a little scruffy just now, but the times we flew together, they're polished silver within.

I chattered away to Dan about those days, how the T's air conditioning system would throw little snowballs over the pilot's shoulders, full throttle go-around on humid days; how reliable and honest was this airplane, how one needed to be sure the tiptank fuel caps were tight before takeoff (if they weren't she'd siphon all the fuel out of one tank and not the other leaving you in a pretty pickle, wildly out of balance); what happened if a pilot taxied the airplane too slowly into a turn and cocked the nosewheel crosswise on the taxiway (what happened is it took full throttle and the pilot standing on one brake to straighten the wheel, meanwhile blowing all unchained objects in his engine jetblast well over the horizon).

And here she is on her pedestal, barely half a century later. Those times bright, all of a sudden I realized I must be sounding to Dan like an old-time pilot once sounded to me. "Well, son, our Sopwith Camel, she had that rotary engine, and she could turn like absolute crazy to the left, there was no Fokker in all the Richthofen Circus could follow your Camel in a left turn. 'Course you had to see 'em coming, the Circus. They were awful good at not being seen till they were right on you ..."

They're history, the planes I flew: F-84's and F-86's, even the F-100's, they were the newest fighters, called the "Century Series" then: the '100, '101,

'102, '104, '105, '106. So brand new they were secret aircraft, today they're frozen on their display pedestals, canopies gone blank, intakes sealed.

Odd the way things get old, on this planet, but spirits don't. Feels odd because it's yesterday, it's the flick of a thought, and those aircraft are alive again. I can tell you where the fuel counter of that T-33 is located, tell the rumble of the engine lighting off on start, tell what airspeed to carry down final approach in your F-84F (it's 140 knots plus five knots for every thousand pounds of fuel remaining over two thousand pounds), say the feel in the airplane when you press the ATO button to fire those four rocket boosters on takeoff.

Metal bodies on pedestals, elevated graves; spirits yet living in dreams of old flights and of the kids who once stepped into their cockpits, lit their fires, signaled thumbs-out to the ground crew—chocks away.

Not a tear this morning; why these as I write?

CHAPTER 39

Maintenance Day and a Surprise Visit

Ronnie Robbins runs the maintenance hangar at Plainview Airport. He's one of those folks one instantly likes, the first half-second on meeting. Forty years he's been working on airplanes, flying them, rebuilding them so they fly again. On the wall of one of Ronnie's hangars, as far from the sea as it is possible to get, look who slips into our world of appearances: Granma Cat!

Her memory of flights past is with her still, I'll bet, as vivid as mine. There's a way, isn't there, of making her living memory our own, if we want it to be, if we value the lessons she's learned and chooses to share? I expect the answer is of course. I expect we'll see examples still to come, on this journey with the two Little Cats.

Today was all maintenance, till late, till just an hour ago. But in this one day, Dan had replaced the carburetor, found a problem and fixed it in the other carburetor (this engine has two of them), replaced the spark plugs, replaced the tailwheel assembly, invented a system to keep freak failures from attacking his landing gear and then test-flew Jennifer in the sunset. End of daylight, she's flying perfectly.

Tomorrow we plan to be on our way early in the morning, a curvi-wandering route toward north New Mexico.

It's already late and my belief is that I must sleep, this quick page all in haste but I wanted you to feel the surprise of Granma Cat, same as we felt it, reminding she's with us along the way.

Please calculate the odds of our finding that reminder.

CHAPTER 40

Swords in the Water, and Subjective Flying

We were off at 7:30 a.m., wheels lifting from the runway at Plainview. The wheels keep spinning after one leaves the runway, long after they're retracted. If it bothers, squeeze the brake handle.

We turned west, though air like brushed satin. Let go the controls, our airplanes flew themselves, north and west toward the high country.

At first the land beneath us was intensively cared for, no sign of wilderness so far as one could see:

Gliding on that silk, though, the country slid under us like a great earthen wedge, lifting both airplanes higher, butterflies in sunlight. Within the hour it was just the opposite, we flew over wilderness, no sign of civilization, so far as one could see.

I felt the chill in the air as we climbed. At six thousand feet, it was pretty cold, I thought. At seven thousand, it was very pretty cold. Yet by that time, descending back to six thousand would have put us several hundred feet underground. Cold I preferred.

Puff was setting new personal altitude records every few minutes. She would nearly quadruple her record by the time we landed, but she was learning to wear experience lightly, an invisible cloak, tossed casual over her wing. Some days we set records, some days we don't.

Then came along the sight upon which Dan and I agreed. Water.

"Wheels up ..." he called and dived toward a turquoise jewel set midst the dangerous unmoving land.

Conchas Lake rests at 4200 feet MSL (mean sea level), and as Mister Worry, I was wondering if we landed would we be able to take off again, in the thin air? Dan had no questions, since he's done this before. So we landed, two trans-con ducks happy to get their feathers wet after days of dry.

So comforting. I felt Puff relax and enjoy the moment, after all that Hard and Sharp beneath her wings. The two seaplanes drifted side by side for a few minutes, the water in front of Jennifer wide and clear, the way

before me and Puff, it had a field of slender reeds some hundreds of feet in front of us. Reeds are no problem, we'd slide right through them.

Then Dan and Jennifer were enveloped in spray and power as they began their takeoff.

Let's do it, Puff!

I pressed the throttle full open and she surged ahead, though not nearly so quickly as she does at sea level. Skimming the water, 30 mph lifted to become 35, the reeds sweeping toward us.

It was at that moment that I saw those are not reeds, ahead, those are trees! … those are brittle hard sharp mesquite trees! Void of leaves, drowned when the river dammed to make this lake, branches like sword-blades. Swords closing swiftly ahead, Puff would be hash if she struck them. At 40 mph they were on us. I snatched the control stick back. "Fly, Puff! You've got to fly!"

Which she did. Sooner than ever I had forced her off the water in practice, she lifted, startled, streaked inches over the sharp-as-steel blades, me waiting the screeching clawing drag of them on her body. Waiting was all that came. No sound but Puff's engine screaming wide open, struggling to fly and slowly slowly gaining speed. At 50 mph we had it made, I eased her nose ever so slightly down and we saw 55 … 60, 61 mph, and climbing.

I breathed again, felt a rush of love and joy, awe for this dear creature, the one who had just saved our lives, flying when she could not have flown.

Puff, thank you.

Swords in the Water, and Subjective Flying

Piece of cake, she said, panting. I felt her proud little smile.

Damn it, Richard, I thought, those were not reeds those were trees! Assume nothing on takeoff, Assume Nothing!

We climbed back up to altitude, me chastened, Puff thinking no-problem. The altitude we were going for was High As We Could Get, back deep into the cold. In minutes I was shivering again.

Why did I feel the cold? Because I am not a geologist. To me, the rocks below were hard, sharp, even pretty in a colorful, cruel way. The rock, the land, was to be avoided by fragile mortals flying fragile aircraft. The ice of altitude crept into my bloodstream, sharper every few hundred feet we gained. Not being a geologist, I was looking constantly for clear places to land, should the engine fail. There's a trail, maybe a wild-horse trail, but if we had to land I'd set her wheels down right ... there ...

Not two hundred feet away Dan was having a different flight. He was not cold. He was swept away by the earth unfolding beneath us: rifts and clines, high gneisses and ranges of mountains ground to level dust by waters while new mountains burst up from beneath no one knows how. He was fired by adrenaline, I was chilled, pre-living engine failures.

Whom do you suppose learned the most, who most enjoyed that three and a half hours in the air?

The minute we landed at Las Vegas (New Mexico, not Nevada), elevation 6,877 feet above sea level, I was dragging out my snowmobile suit, grateful for the extra layers, while Dan chirped happily in his shirtsleeves, did I see the colors of that last escarpment, feel the wonder of it? Did I know what had to happen to slice the rock away from the face of it?

My answers, unfortunately, were no, no, and no, tucking my scarf into my collar.

Subjective flying, it was, so powerful it changed our inner temperatures. Perhaps all flying is subjective. Flying with someone terrified of airplanes, I can feel the clash of our two attitudes: Don't you love the freedom of the sky/ How soon can I land and get my feet on the ground? Doesn't happen often, since birds of a feather rarely flock with, say, armadillos.

On our way once again, I was clawing for altitude, Dan loving every minute, every view of earth like boiling honey, a few million years per bubble.

By afternoon the thermals were lighting off as the ground heated. We rode them up to heights the airplanes could only have reached after long

hauls through still air. Sometimes gentle lift, sometimes nearly explosive, our wings shuddering in the force of them. At one point the lift was enough to throw Puff nearly to ten thousand feet.

The dial on the right, the vertical speed indicator, shows we're going up just under 1300 feet per minute. There are downdrafts, too, so one slows in the lift, to gain altitude, and dives through the sink to get through it fast.

Then Dan was on the radio to the control tower at Farmington. Rare event, the tower gave us a downwind runway, asked us to land with the wind on our tail, pushing us fast along the ground. Dan waited patiently. In a

Swords in the Water, and Subjective Flying

minute the tower operator corrected himself, gave us clearance for a proper runway, into the wind, and we landed.

The little Cats covered and tied for the night, Dan to his photographs, me to my keyboard, sharing this adventure with you.

Now I sleep, for we have an early takeoff tomorrow to some of the most spectacular geology (and waters) in this country.

Good night, Puff. Thank you for our lives.

CHAPTER *41*

Practical Precognition

*d*knew this picture was going to be taken, days before the shutter clicked. Exactly this picture.

Certain things come true because it is their nature to come true. Dan Nickens is your geologist's Indiana Jones. Others of that calling are content to examine their shales and limestones and igneous shards, examine them spec-imen by bagged specimen,

they're happy at the controls of their electron microscope.

My flying partner, I knew it from the start: he prefers his geology to be blurring a few feet beneath his airplane, to examine it from such a position that a wrong turn would be a spectacular ending to his career. He didn't tell me this, I saw it in the way he flies his seaplane.

In the military, they call it a CR, which is short for calculated risk. This means that when one makes this choice or that one, everything will probably work out fine. It's understood, though, that once in a hundred times, or once in ten, things may go wrong and one will find himself or herself in a challenging situation at best and not alive at worst.

Jennifer's engine has been running as smoothly as a sewing machine's for the last two days. Odds are that it will continue to purr along for another hour without failing. If it fails, however, the only place for Indiana to land is in the river below, complete with jagged stone, white-water rapids, and most likely Undiscovered River Spiders, mean little guys and deadly poison.

I took the picture while flying Puff safely above the canyon rim, away from the chasm the river has cut into rock over the last 20 million years or so. If Puff's engine stopped right now, we would land all comfortable in a level patch of sand or rock high above the river. I would rest and enjoy a cookie, then repair the engine and we would fly along our way.

The chasm between my cautious mind and Indiana's inquisitive one is deeper than the gorge bounding Jennifer's wings with solid rock, and that's how I knew days ago that I would be taking this photograph. It is characteristic of me to have a backup plan if things go wrong. It is characteristic of Dan to accept a more adventurous Plan B than mine.

"If the engine stops," Dan would say, "no worries! I land on the river, and shoot the rapids in the SeaRey! Fifty miles downstream the river widens, I paddle to the nearest comfortable shore, fix the engine and take off!"

You want to ask about his chances of survival, running fifty miles of rapids in the shell of a seaplane, but you don't because if you're counseling caution Indy's just going to smile at you, a sympathetic smile—poor armchair geologist, you're missing the adventure of science!

He followed the river this way for nearly an hour. Jennifer's engine did not fail, so Indiana has an understanding of living geology which no other scientist shares.

Me, I'm a flyer, and intend to remain so. For me, C.R. stands for Colorado River, seen from a conservative distance from aboard Puff as from aboard a flying armchair, cookie in one hand, magnifying glass in the other.

Oddly enough, we get along just fine. Dan does not mind my living as I choose, I don't squeak about his choices. I don't know what I offer him, but here's one sight he offered me, that I would never have known, had I not been flying with Indiana:

We get closer, it gets bigger:

We circled the rock (once buried 3,000 feet underground, Dan told me), now emerged by millions of years' eroding of everything else above and around. At close range, albeit without touching, Ship Rock looked hard indeed.

These sites, Ship Rock and Monument Valley and the Goosenecks all passed below, on a route of adventure once scary to think about, today a part of Puff's History of Scary Things Overcome.

Practical Precognition

Such is the power of our interests and loves. Without knowing, we touch and change the lives of others through our own choice of passions and the pleasures we derive. So did Indiana's choice touch Puff and me.

From Dan's CR to the other C.R. we flew. Soon as the river widened, Dan called, "Gear up …" Jennifer's nose dropped down toward the water at a bend in the river, a wide place, and blue.

Puff was anxious to touch water again, and in less than a minute we were gear up flaps down boost pump on, listening to the familiar happy sigh of water lightly on our keel. We swung in a wide speedboat step turn and joined Jennifer heading toward the beach.

"I'll take one side, you take the other," Dan called, for there ahead was a double cove, the river clear as emerald around. "Look out for rocks underwater."

This was easy to do, for I could see to the bottom as we taxied slow now, on the surface. Rocks there were, deep below.

Puff's bow crunched lightly on the sand and I shut her engine down into a blanket of silence. Not a soul in sight, the river itself not making a sound.

Dan set a rock table with cookies for his lunch, I brought my granola bar. "This is nice," someone said. From the hillside, some photos:

It works, I thought. Puff can take me to any place, almost, any secret land we can find together from the air. One of the few aircraft built for landing away from airports as much as on them, she's the perfect intimate flying companion.

Practical Precognition

We breathed the delicious peace of that beach for an hour. One could stay here, I thought, bring a tent, a star map, a hand-cranked computer … one could stay there for a long glad time, indeed.

We landed at Page, Arizona for the eve, and I write these lines. Practical precognition. I knew this would come true in my life, because I planned it, loved it, worked a year for it to happen. One doesn't need to be psychic to see these things true, long before they happen.

Travels with *Puff*

CHAPTER 42

Exploring Big Water

Did I know yon mountainside is not igneous, but metamorphic? No, but I found out today that it is.

Anybody with an aircraft radio scanner along our way was getting a free education in practical geology. I hadn't paid much attention till this voyage across the continent, but now it strikes me ... this entire country (and by now I wouldn't be surprised to find that the whole world) is made out of rock!

And all that rock? It's moving!

We were flying along, our two little SeaReys, and all of a sudden up ahead and to our left, this!

One minute I looked ahead and everything was dead level. The next minute there's this big cloud of dust and the block of mountain six miles wide it's come roaring up from below like it couldn't hold its breath a half-second longer and had to get some air.

My friend Indiana and his talking about things that take millions of years to happen: now I see 'em and it looks like seconds, like we have to dodge this erupting subsiding shift-sliding-disappearing earth we've been perched on for the last microsecond or so.

He's quick to say that big things happen that geologists don't have a clue why. The Rocky Mountains, for instance. We have to fly over 'em but nobody knows why they're there. No tectonic plates shifting below, all that rock just decided one day to hop up ten thousand, thirteen thousand feet into the air. On a whim, apparently, and if you happen to be flying a little puff of a seaplane, you'd best be careful lest one like the one in the picture doesn't hop to thirteen thousand while you're cruising at five. Lucky for us we were higher than this one when it blew.

And listen to this: Your common glass of table water, it isn't really water. Another name for it is hydroxic acid (honest!) and it is the most implacable cutter and tearer-downer of rock the world has ever known. Look below, what a single glass of hydroxic-acid water, magnified several hundred trillion times, did to this dead-flat table land:

Given a hundred million years, the stuff can dissolve anything!

Nevertheless, we mortals love to mess with danger, so Puff and Jennifer homed in on the biggest mass of Danger northwest of the Pecos: Lake Mead. With the intention, mind you, that we were going to splash down in a sea of hydroxic acid!

We were following the Colorado River, approaching the northern stem of the lake, when Dan called, "You're leader. Go explore!"

Having been here before, I guessed, he wanted to see the lake with new eyes, perhaps Puff and I would explore a place he hadn't found. We found one within minutes. From the air, it looked as if it could be a gentle haven, clear water and a spice-color beach.

"Wheels up for a water landing," I called. Wheels double-checked up, boost pump on flaps down throttle back. The water was glassy, normally a challenge for seaplanes, but there was a shore nearby for altitude reference and I thought nothing of it. As we neared the water I triple-checked the gear up and by the time I had turned back to the lake, we struck the surface. We didn't hit hard, but getting distracted when landing is not professional and leads to a bounce or ten on landing.

Dan was not distracted, made as pretty a touchdown as ever I've seen.

This is one of the rewards of the light seaplane flyer and his or her airplane, the chance to stop here:

Off we went exploring again, to find this place:
And this:

The winds came up in the afternoon, but only in the narrow gorges between sections of the lake. It's scary to get caught in a downdraft 500 feet per minute when you're 100 feet above the water. As though the wind intended to remind us that she does her share of rock-eroding, too.

Early flight tomorrow, to Death Valley, we think.

Remember that part about Dan being crazy about geology? Is it true that without a passion for something, doesn't matter what, something we love to do or to be around or submerge ourselves in, we're doomed to lives of boredom, we get the leftovers from the ones who love their something?

So far as I can tell, that's so.

CHAPTER 43

Exploring Big Sand

Do you have a taste for carrot cake?

There's a restaurant in the hotel in Boulder City, Nevada (I've forgotten the name I think it has "Railroad" in it) surrounded by slot machines in which after dinner if you say you'd like a taste of dessert they serve you a six- or eight-layer carrot cake about the size of a pumpkin. You take the seven-eighths of the pumpkin leftover with you to your room, though at 6 am next morning it may no longer be what you had in mind on which to start your day.

So it was with me and Dan. We continued our journey carrot-cake-less, as how would you feel to have an engine failure in the middle of Death Valley and they find you fifty years later with a petrified cake in your hand?

We did take extra water, as in case of a forced landing we would find ourselves in what the military calls a "survival situation."

We were airborne as early as the opening of the fixed-base operator would allow.

It still feels odd to me, to see Puff and Jennifer, these wilderness creatures, on a busy modern airport:

We left quick as we could, Dan carrying five gallons of fuel in the cockpit with him as our destination, the Furnace Creek airport in Death Valley, has no fuel available.

The air was warm turning cool as we climbed, but it didn't look all that cool outside.

I happened to be leader at the time, when I heard Dan call. "This is too good to miss!" and all at once Jennifer went wild-spiraling down, throwing away our hard-won altitude for this:

Dan will have some photos tonight, I thought.

Death Valley is some 250 feet below sea level. Down there strange things happen, bonkers-things happen. Puff's shadow took that moment to break loose on its own again. She's sometimes forgotten to bring her shadow when she flies, or it's missing when we're ready to go … this is the first time I've seen it leave us behind, rush on to Furnace Creek ahead of her.

Puff? I asked, Your shadow? Do you know what it's doing now?

I know. Can't help it. Mind of its own.

Dan didn't notice. He was studying geology, a classroom like nowhere in the world. Recognize this, from your studies?

Dan explained it to me on the radio, unconcerned there was no way for us to sustain life in that silicated, desiccated world if we were forced down. Survival is not a geologist's concern. These mountains are not being covered in sand, can you forget about surviving and notice … they are not being covered in sand, they are lifting up through it!

About that time, around the moment we were in the center of this lifeless albeit abounding in fascinating rock sand and a million tons of Dry, my so-called Navigation Aid failed. Instead of this neat moving map with a little airplane at my position, it went blank. Pouting, I suppose, that it ran out of its so-precious Electricity when the fitting that hosed in those electrons burnt itself out.

According to my gas station road map, however, Furnace Creek ought to be about ... there, out of sight now but right spang off that range of lifeless mountains up ahead I hope.

Dan just plain didn't care. In that hour what sane person would care about getting lost in the middle of Death Valley at noon when there is so

much ... rock! to explore? If you will notice how the sedimentary layers, Richard, have rotated, they've been pushed by the Sierra Nevada, fifty miles away!

It felt like flying a movie script, our different priorities, Dan's being some of the most astounding geology in the world, an open book before his eyes; my priority being ... well, staying alive.

My road map was torn and since it covered the whole western United States it didn't have a lot of time for details like where are you in the midst of this desert getting hotter by the minute, but would you care to know where Los Angeles is, or San Francisco, the City by the Bay?

What, I wondered, were we doing with two seaplanes—seaplanes, mind you, in the midst of—this?

Travels with *Puff*

I wanted to press the microphone button, in my delirium, mirages dancing, and ask, "Oh Dan, can't you see that big green tree, and the water running free, and it's waiting there for you and meeee? Water ... Cool, clear, water ..."

But I didn't. I folded the map and looked hard. This way is north, so Furnace Creek must be ...

Puff, I thought, I wonder why they call it "Furnace Creek," instead of, say, "Cool Clear Water Creek?"

My airplane is growing fast, gaining broad experience from her adventures, but sophisticated or subtle she is not.

Because it's burning hot?

Half an hour later, came a little speck of green away out ahead of us. Green!

I stuffed the map away. Fortunately one does not transmit thoughts to one's wingman, who only hears words when a microphone button is pressed.

"SeaRey," I called, "We'll land Runway One Five. Let's go two-two-nine."

"Two," said Dan.

By now you know your air-talk: that Runway One Five is the landing strip that's pointed down the magnetic heading of 150 degrees, sort of southeast, which is where the wind was coming from and into which we wanted to land as we always land into the wind or as nearly to into it as we can. The two-two-nine comment was to the radio frequency that air traffic uses at the Furnace Creek Airport: 122.9 megacycles (all right: "megaHertz," about as awkward a way to honor Mister Hertz as can be imagined).

Dan said, "Two," to let me know that the number two aircraft (namely himself and Jennifer) in our formation (often called a "flight," as in "A flight of two aircraft"), understood what to do, so that he didn't need to say, "Roger," which means the same thing. He could have said, "Roger," but that would not have been as correct a response as "Two," in this rather formal transmission.

After I switched to the new frequency, I pressed the button and said, "Lead," (pronounced Leed, as in Leeder). Dan said, "Two," to let me know he had switched frequencies as requested and we were on the same radio channel again.

At which point I broadcast to any airplanes which might be in the Furnace Creek airport traffic pattern (in the middle of one of the world's major

deserts ha-ha), "Furnace Creek traffic, SeaRey Three Four Six Papa Echo, flight of two SeaReys, two miles southeast we'll be a left downwind Runway One Five Furnace Creek."

Redundant, deliberately saying "Furnace Creek" twice since it's possible another aircraft came on frequency a split second after I began my position report and didn't know which airport we were landing at and therefore whether to look out for us or not.

The odds of this happening today were shall we say low.

Wheels down for a land landing, flaps down, boost pump on … that familiar checklist. I slid back the canopy hatches to catch the last of the cooler higher air, pulled the throttle back to idle power and turned to land.

In that instant I saw a flash of dark and heard _VAM!_ Something had hit the airplane!

Not a clue what could have hit us or how badly we were damaged, I checked the wheels down, to make sure one hadn't ripped off. Power doesn't matter we're high enough we don't need power to reach the runway, Richard, no need to think about what the VAM! was, all that matters is this landing, you've got it made.

Not a cry, not a word from Puff.

If this were the movie *Top Gun*, the script would have me pressing the microphone button and screaming for help, 'way the most useless thing a pilot can do but scriptwriters love it in air movies. Fortunately I am not

Travels with *Puff*

in *Top Gun* I am landing at Furnace Creek, the runway is clear and broad ahead and below. Just fly the airplane, glide it down, gently, gently touch the tailwheel first ...

and squeak-squeak from the tires and Puff was rolling straight down the centerline. Whatever we hit, it didn't wreck the landing gear.

We taxied in and shut our engines down. Out of the cockpit, I checked Puff over for signs of collision. Not a mark. Not a scratch, anywhere.

What was going on? I puzzled about this, reached for a cookie from the cookie-bag while I considered the mystery.

Something was different about the cockpit. At first I sloughed it off ... what could possibly have changed about the cockpit in which I have been sitting for the last two weeks?

My snowsuit. That was what changed. My black snowsuit was missing.

It had been stuffed into the baggage space behind the right seat, now it was gone.

Canopy hatch slid open to get the cool air, turning down to land ... my snowsuit saw its chance in the sudden rush of wind through the cockpit and yearning a life without cold, it had bailed out! That was the dark flash I saw, and the VAM! had been the propeller whipping into the fabric, a sleeve or a leg, as the me-shaped sleeping bag burst out of the airplane.

Dan was not far away, pouring his two cans of gasoline into Jennifer's tank.

I walked over, shaking my head. "Dan, you won't believe what happened!"

"What happened?" My wingman and geology instructor was ready for me to say anything. Since Richard is alive and Puff undamaged, it couldn't be anything serious. Could he be about to tell me he had seen a metamorphic upthrust, he thought, which I may have missed, or a cline, mostly covered in sand?

"My snowsuit! I was turning base to final and the wind ... it blew out of the airplane!"

"Did it hit ... is Puff OK?"

When the fuel was poured, we walked to my airplane.

"She looks fine," I said.

"Maybe," then, "Look here. The tip of the propeller."

There it was, one corner of one tip of one blade, an abrasion a quarter-inch wide. To which was yet attached a single black thread:

Was anyone watching from the ground, walking with their granddaughter? What would they have said?

"Look, Charlotte, there's a cute little airplane, about to land. Don't see many landing here, do we? Wonder where it came from, where it's … *the pilot just fell out!* Don't look, oh the poor man's drifting down into the cactus and that cute little airplane it's landing by itself!"

Appearances: Sometimes bizarre, always misleading. Don't you dare take them for real, dear observer.

If you'd care to have a free snowsuit, by the way, it's waiting for you, only one thread missing, somewhere under the base leg of the approach to Runway One Five at Furnace Creek Airport, Death Valley California, USA.

I'll take my chances with freezing days ahead, and decided to leave the snowsuit for you, on your next visit to the Valley, while Dan and I press ahead for Bishop, just an hour-plus northwest.

There were some fairly high ridges to cross, so we were kind of struggling to climb as much as possible, using thermals now and then, remembering all I once knew about soaring. Turns out I was the one struggling, Dan was enjoying the geology.

"By that sand dune at nine o'clock low, see the road? If you want to do an off-airport landing …"

"I'm working hard for altitude, here," I replied. "I'd rather not dump it all and go land on a road just now."

"Roger." By way of saying, Oh, flying is work, is it now, Richard? You're deciding to pass up this chance to look at a *sand dune!* in order to get a little more altitude to cross a ridge that you know we're going to cross anyhow one way or the other? Pity your soul!

But I was being too grown-up to play: if the wind is from the southeast, then it'll be updrafts on the southeast side of the ridge, downdrafts on the northwest side. Don't even think about flying the northwest side. Work this thermal, worrrrk it … Slide now to the southeast side of the peaks, here.

A wide green square appeared, the color of shade trees, not ten miles distant as we topped the ridge: Bishop, California.

Cautiously I picked my way amid the family of mini-peaks below, waiting any second for downdrafts should I strive too quickly. Running out of lift, or hitting downdrafts when one is in mountain country, that isn't anybody's idea of fun.

When I had the airport made ... that is, when I could land even if the wheels fell off or the engine stopped, I deliberately moved into what I knew would be the northwest-side downdrafts near the ridges behind. I wanted to test my knowledge, see if I was right.

Too bad for my knowledge, there were no downdrafts on the north side of the ridges. No downdrafts, no updrafts, no nothin'.

All that concern about being dragged down, wasted. Am I too cautious with my life as well, I thought, concerned about downdrafts which never happen, flying my choices way too carefully? Which almost never happen.

Funny, how the metaphors of the calling we choose can ask such pointed questions about our way of life.

Am I living too cautiously? Would I change if I could?

I can change. I need to think about that. Maybe I need a motorcycle.

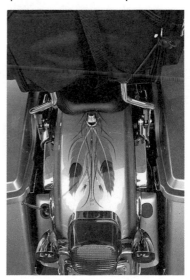

No sooner had I written these words in my hotel room than I went to the hotel lobby to find two men dressed in motorcycle leathers, checking in for the night.

Odd that they should be on their way across the country on their Harleys, just as Dan and I are on our way across it in our SeaReys.

I asked if I could take their picture, and when they went off to their rooms, and as I was leaving I took a last look at the leader's machine. Painted on the rear fender:

Will someone please tell me what's going on, this trip?

CHAPTER 44

Takeoff, and Freedom Found

Each day, for Dan and me on our journey across the continent, begins like this: The two SeaReys parked side by side, Leader looks to wingman sitting quiet in his cockpit. Wingman nods: I'm ready for engine start. Leader nods OK, touches the engine start switch. Same instant, wingman touches his own starter. There's a twin soft purr of propellers on the flight line: our day has begun.

Almost always there's no destination we must reach, no heading and altitude we must hold, no briefing says Dan's leader today or Richard is. What we have is we generally agree on the approximate direction we're heading, and we'll land maybe somewhere that looks inviting, and now and then for fuel.

Today's flight was yesterday's agreement: our Geologist's-Dream Air Safari and Gentle Cross-Country Adventure ought include a circuit of Mono Lake, filled chock-a-block with natural wonders like tufa and lava and brine shrimp, then wherever came after that, all it had to be was north.

Dan turned out to be flight leader by virtue of he's got the camera—I'm leader when Puff's ready for her close-up, and he flies Jennifer as required to get the picture he wants. From Bishop there wouldn't be pictures but a long climb to altitude, since Mono is surrounded by high country, so Dan was leader.

189

While he navigated, the sky going darker as we climbed, Puff took the chance to nail her altitude record above ten thousand feet:

She will place this on the wall of her hangar next her 100-feet-below-sea-level record from yesterday's Death Valley jaunt:

The difference in airspeed has something to do with the density of the air, but that's a story for you to explore as you get your Sport Pilot's license.

Puff stayed up at altitude, watched Dan and Jennifer play down among the tufa towers, of which I had never heard and for which Mono Lake is famous to everybody else.

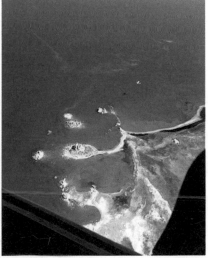

Dan was aloft in Geologist Heaven—who else is using his airplane to study stone? When I innocently estimated that by now he must have a thousand photos of rocks and Puff along the way, he looked at me pityingly: "A thousand?" I didn't want to compound my out-of-it-ness by asking, so I suppose he's got fifty thousand photos on this trip for his book which ought to be titled *Jennifer's Living Geology: A Handbook for Small Amphibian Airplanes*. That may not be quite the title, but I'm ready to be floored by the photos.

Of course he had to touch down on the surface of that strange lake, just touch it and fly again. If he had stopped on the water, at that altitude, Jennifer could not have taken off again till the air went much colder.

This is the real color of the water where they touched, by the way. I just held my phone-camera out the window and clicked:

After a while, Dan called Puff down for her glamour-shots in the Land of Odd that is Mono Lake.

Don't let me touch the … water, please.

It's a strange feeling, flying there. Strange as in creepy, weird, dead. There are no fish in the lake, Dan said, but millions of brine shrimp, supper for seagulls. And Mono is supposed to be a water supply for the city of Los Angeles. Hm.

We flew around a volcano vent or whatever it's called, in which the lava had been tumbled in blocks. I have not yet been able to stump Dan with my questions on how can the earth possibly do rocks like that, but I'll guess lava-blocks have to come from earthquakes and I'd guess large earthquakes of the sort human beings have never witnessed.

I've never had more than a passing interest in geology, but this flight with a man who has such passion for it is getting me fascinated.

I've thought of rock as, well, rock-like: hard, unyielding: bonk-bonk. Not so. Watch it on a newsreel of millions of years, Dan says, or watch it

Travels with *Puff*

deep beneath the crust, and rock is liquid, plastic, curving, twisting, bubbling. Look at it from altitude, you can see solid ground rippling away like water from crust-plates crashing together, splashing mountains all directions. I'm waiting in line for Jennifer's book.

By the time our photo shoot was over, the land was warming and we became pretend-sailplanes looking for lift to get out of the monster soup-bowl that holds the lake. On her own at that altitude and temperature, a SeaRey can climb a few hundred feet per minute … she's near what they call her service ceiling, about as high as she can go unaided. But we found today that aided by columns of rising air, a 'Rey can climb more than a thousand feet per minute. She can also lose altitude that fast in falling airs, so it was a dance we did, changing partners with air columns till we were over the rim to lower country.

Relatively lower. We reached Walker Lake after half an hour's flying through rough air. Density altitude was 6,000 feet, and we chatted on our private radio channel:

"Elevation's four thousand, Dan, but the density's six. No wind, or not much. Can we take off again if we land?"

"Don't know. Let's try it. I'll try it first, see if Jennifer can do it."

"If she can't, we'll land too and camp the night. Fly off in the cool air tomorrow?"

"Sounds like a plan."

"Then I'll go first. See how Puff likes western high altitude."

"You've got it."

We've got it, Puff, I told her. Let's have a little splash.

She was keen for the adventure, sure she could take off again. It's a pretty lake.

I agreed. Walker has none of the eerie vampire-ness of Mono. The water was blue-green, sparkling colors and clear.

"Wheels up for the water."

I checked the wheels up for the millionth time, slowed Puff to 60 mph, flaps down, boost pump on, turned down into the wind. In a few seconds the wavelets were whipping by inches beneath us, then the juddering hiss as Puff's keel touched down. She slid graceful to a stop, floating calm and sweet, while Jennifer came sweeping by on the step.

Now, my Puffly, I thought, Let's see if you can take off again.

Piece of cake.

The throttle came ahead to takeoff power, yet for a few seconds Puff didn't react, as though she were startled by how thin the air is, here. Then she moved, but plowed through the water instead of leaping on top of it.

I pushed the control stick full forward, a trick that Dan had suggested for high-altitude takeoffs, and sure enough, Puff went lighter, picked up speed, spray beginning to fly. Then she sort of shook her head and got serious about this project. With that, she was all at once lifted from plowing the water to skimming the top of it, and after that there was no doubt that she would fly. It was a long takeoff slide, for her, but finally the wavelets were barely flickering on her keel, and we were in the air.

"Good girl, Puff!" I said it aloud, I believe, as when I fly alone with her I'm not sure when I speak to her and when I think to her. All the same to Puff. She was pleased with herself, her chance to show Jennifer how it's done. I felt her big sister noticing. *Good job, Puff!*

"Wheels up for the water," Dan called, and as we climbed and turned, he and Jennifer descended. What a lovely sight that is from the air, his little 'Rey, touching down.

We landed again, close by Jennifer, as she taxied toward shore. We taxied too, and I watched through six feet or so, clear water to the bottom. Sand it was, with bits of broken sandstone scattered there (not sandstone, Dan told me later, it's caliche). The water went shallower, and clearer. I noticed that Jennifer, ahead of us, had stopped, her engine shut down a hundred feet from shore.

A second later I felt a bump as Puff's keel touched sand, then another. We were farther from shore than Jennifer, but with a final sliding stop Puff said this is as far as we go.

"Thank you, Little Cat," I said, and before she could protest that was Jennifer and not her, switched her engine off.

Travels with *Puff*

It was totally silent, save for the lap of waves against Puff's hull. As I unfastened my shoulder harness, took off the headset, I noticed that Dan was out of his cockpit, wading to shore. He moved unsteadily, as though he were sinking in mud with every step.

In a minute, I found that's exactly what he was doing. I sank eight inches in the thick stuff every few steps. I could pull my feet out of it, but not my water-shoes, which stayed buried there. Finally found those and pulled 'em loose, made it in a tottering walk to shore.

I stood there, watching the wide empty lake and our two airplanes.

We four were the only living creatures in sight, miles around every direction.

Dan and I looked at the sight, at each other, and then we began to laugh. The laugh, it had happened before in the same

situation: are we the only two crazy nuts in all the world, to come out here to the center of nowhere, no other soul for fifty-hundred miles round?

Answer: Yes.

What it felt besides funny, was free. We had nobody's permission but our own, and needed no other, to follow what we each most loved to do with our lives, which at that moment was to stand on this beach forsaken by every other human being. No footprints, no tire tracks,  no nothin' but us four friends in the sunlight, clear cool water rippling like high-speed transparent rock while we stood nearby.

We laughed for that freedom. How much study and work and cash and loving effort we had taken, giving priority to these little airplanes and to practicing our flying skills, and now we stood free on a desert lakeside that could be any waterside anywhere in the world, if we chose to be there.

By that moment I had spent over a hundred hours in Puff's little cockpit, flying, we had made hundreds of water landings. Scared ourselves now and then, laughed alone in the sky and now with a friend who had made the same choices, sacrificed other possibilities to make this one come true. No golf, no bowling, no sports events, no drinking or card games with buddies on Saturday night. Gave it all up. To stand where we are standing. Now.

And that, somehow, is so funny that one laughs out loud, for the joy of it.

From Walker Lake it was half an hour to another Nevada lake, this one

 with people here and there, dots on the beach, a sparse few boats on the water but not in sight when we came ashore.

We called it a day at Carson City, put the airplanes to bed at the airport, were offered and accepted a ride from a local pilot on his way home for the day.

Now it's two a.m. There's no sound in the room, but I'm still laughing.

Travels with *Puff*

CHAPTER 45

Only a Hundred Miles, and What an Only

The forecast was not wonderful: winds to 25 knots on the north part of our journey. Those winds over rugged terrain would be less than fun for us, still we hear the old pilot's adage: Never cancel on a forecast.

The prudent course: take off and see what it's like, land if it isn't pretty. Which we did, Dan and Jennifer leading as we climbed from Carson City over Reno, Nevada.

I once lived in Reno, a quiet, pretty town and if you like flashy lights, there's a place for that, too.

We were two prospectors from a different time, crossing the high-tech Class C airspace over the city, but hey, what are radios for?

By 10 a.m., the smooth air was giving way to a few thermals, bouncing us a bit and saying wait till afternoon. Big talk, thermals. Come afternoon, good luck finding us.

Off the controller's radar, Puff and I took the lead, calculating fuel load and distance to fly and what the weather might be ahead and if it were such as to make us unhappy such as thunderstorms and high winds what options would I have and I don't care for those I'd rather divert to Susanville.

"How's Susanville?" I called to Dan.

"Agree." He'd been doing some calculating of his own.

Since Susanville was no more than sixty miles away, Puff dropped down toward Pyramid Lake, a bright liquid jewel on the high desert, magnet for small seaplanes.

"Feel like landing?" I called. Water liquid turquoise, shore rocky.

"I'm wingman," he said, tossing decision back to me.

"Wheels up for the water," I replied.

The water, after so much desert, is so deliciously ... wet!

Wind calm, water smooth, what a pleasure it is to feel Puff splashing happily down, that sun-glare spray diamonding everywhere, tossing drops in the cockpit, over me. I licked them from my lips. Delicious; water clear enough we floated in transparent color.

Then off again, out toward a remoter part, with what looked like islands but weren't. We flew low over these, and Dan called, "A tent! Do you see the tent?"

I wondered why my silent wingman should sound so enthusiastic about a camper's shelter. Somebody wants to be alone.

"Make a ninety-two-seventy," he called. "Look at that!"

What kind of a wingman gives commands to his leader? Ah, I realized. Not a wingman. A geologist. Dan has found something scientifically remarkable on the surface.

A turn of 90 degrees in one direction followed by a turn of 270 degrees in the other will bring you in the opposite direction precisely over the point where you started, and we were precisely over something major neat.

I did as instructed, and in that place, coming from the ground, a feather of steam blowing thirty feet high! Not a tent, Dan had said, a *vent!*

Jennifer had already splashed down, Puff and I turned to follow. Wheels up for a water landing. Flaps, boost pump. What has he found?

Next minute Puff's bow was scraping on the sand, stopping in water clear as air.

How can this place be so isolated? Why aren't there hotels here, bright umbrellas dotting the beach?

The reason why is that there is many a place on our planet which remains undiscovered by civilization.

We walked over the grass toward the vent, the sound of it a steam locomotive at the station ready to move. It wasn't a periodic geyser we saw, but a continuous one, round-the-clock steam and spray hissing and whuffling, whooshing boiling water fire-hoselike upward.

It is doing this with nobody around to watch, I thought, although we filled that slot for half an hour and I couldn't be certain it would continue after we left. I asked Dan if the water from the geyser, which ran in a stream down to the lake, was drinkable.

"It contains dissolved salts."

"But can I drink it?"

"If you like the taste of sulphur."

Thunderstorms were afoot, so after we had a few hundred photos we were on our way. We landed at Susanville before the storms, tied and covered the airplanes.

How fascinating, I thought, that we've been led through all these adventures, and nothing's harmed us, nothing's shown us the Dark Side of the Force.

You don't believe in the dark side of the Force, something thought to me. At that moment, paying my fuel bill in the office at the Susanville Airport, as far from the ocean as it is possible to get, I glanced above the doorway through which we had entered. This is what I saw:

Finishing it is your job.

Not Granma Cat, but *her* mother, a Douglas Dolphin amphibian airplane, looking down upon Dan and me.

I shall open this sentence and not finish it: "What are the odds, that over the doorway … ?"

CHAPTER 46

Sayin' and Doin'

There's a difference between the two. Sometimes we forget, takes a little reminding once in a while.

Puff has picked up one of my traits, I think: it's easy to say things, promise things, then we're jostled when it's time to make it so. I'll set an appointment, agree to one meeting or another, then time comes to meet and I'll whine, "Why ever did I agree to this? I'd much rather be alone than keeping my promise!"

Puff isn't like me, she doesn't whine. Today, though, it impressed her: running five hours over No Place to Land takes hard work, when the chips are down.

She's such a gifted little airplane, she doesn't blink when I go on about she can land anywhere, she's a STOL airplane (for Short Take Off and Land), whether it's land or water, Puff's safe as a helicopter, without the mass of springs and kettles and such, whirling overhead.

All the way across the country I've been her pilot: where do we land if the engine fails now? And most all the way there's been an answer: here's a river, here's a lake, here's a road, here's a sand-bar, here's a smooth place in the desert it only needs be a couple hundred feet long.

Today it didn't matter if she were a helicopter, today it was hour after hour over trees everywhere. Lose an engine in your helicopter today and you're going down in trees, not much guarantee you're gonna walk away from that landing no matter how good a helicopter, how good an airplane, how good a pilot you are.

Worse for Dan and Jennifer, I was leader today, all day. Their job was to go where I chose, where Puff flew. I decide to fly over trees, Jennifer's engine fails, it's Dan in the trees, Puff and me circling helpless overhead as they go down in a seething ocean of pine.

I could have chosen to stay over roads all the way; I didn't.

We were wheels-up from Susanville at 0730, as we used to say in the military since that sounds more determined and unswerving than 7:30 a.m.

It was forest right away, as Susanville marks the boundary 'tween forest and desert in this part of North California. It is serious, you might say implacable forest:

What cleared places there were, now and then, were steep and logged-over, tree-stumps and slash (what the loggers call the tree-trunks and limbs

they leave on the ground), a field of tank-traps on a wilderness beachhead.

If I've learned one thing in all my days, it's this: *Freedom's a gentle game of life and death.*

No place to land, below.

We're not given freedom, I thought—we take it, whenever we wish. Take freedom and its promise of delicious success, we take as well freedom's bright shadow: the chance of spectacular failure.

Second after minute after hour after hour, Puff's engine's turning five thousand revolutions per minute, three hundred thousand revolutions in one hour, a million and a half revolutions today's flying alone, and we've been flying these last sixteen days, except for Plainview, every single day.

When I pull the propeller through by hand every morning, turning three blades is about one and a half engine revolutions, I pull twelve blades, six revolutions and I feel that, it takes energy.

Puff's engine has fire to help it turn, but those are a lot of revolutions when lives, aircraft and human, depend on the turns.

The little seaplane, she's built for freedom. Tied to the ground, unfree, she's not even alive.

I felt her smile. *Are you?*

Two hours over the forest, our noses pointing west, the Sierra Nevada gradually dropped behind, reluctant to see us go. Once we clung to 8,000 feet to see us over the ridges, wishing it were 10,000, now the ground fell away near Redding, California, and we were way high. Sigh of relief, for not only are the worst of the mountains behind us, there's water ahead! The reservoir north of Redding has over the years slowly been filling … last I flew over, there were fifty feet of bared ground above water level, today it's brim full.

"Wheels up for the water," I called.

"Two."

We turned down in a long sweeping arc, Puff and Jennifer, to a perfect liquid field stretched wide before us, steep slopes and pines towering each side of the water as we touched. Glad fastboats, we held half-power and hushed for a mile along the surface, speed making our snow-path graceful art behind us.

Refreshed by the splash of sea-soul to air-soul, Puff was ready to fly again.

Sayin' and Doin'

A motion of the wrist, throttles pushed a few inches forward, the two sea-planes lifted from the water and climbed away from the planet. Climbing, turning in the shadow and ice of Mt. Shasta.

I had thought to circle the mountain, say hello in the morning, but the closer we came, the more I realized that sort of hello probably wouldn't be said today, for the peak of the mountain lofted far over the highest we could climb. Shasta misses by a few feet being the tallest mountain in the country. At our eight thousand feet a single circle of the giant would add fifty miles to our journey.

Past it we flew, we the size of moths, gliding, wrapped in reverence for the place ... one whispers in the silence of Shasta's heights and snows.

I once lived in this country, too, south of Medford, Oregon, so I played with remembering in the minutes we flew past. Then memory failed, it was new country ahead, unending trees once more.

Puff purred along, not a single miss from her engine, nor had there been one ever, since first we met.

What a dear soul you are, I thought, how close is your spirit to mine. Not one second of this adventure, of this bright whole discovery-of-life would have been possible without you!

I felt her life, gently brushing.

Nor without you.

There's a minute I'll not forget.

This last horizon-wide plain of trees settled, smoothed as though the winds of earth had ceased to blow, the terrain going softer, gentler beneath us near Bandon, Oregon.

Way far out ahead, the horizon was no more rippled and tossed. The horizon was a level smooth line, and it was blue.

This has happened to me before, I thought, how does it feel for Puff? All her life, flying east

brought her to the ocean. Today the ocean's west. In a few minutes, for the first time ever, she will have flown coast to coast.

I felt a quiet joy in her, fascination with the sea turned round, of course, but more a delighted relief, that she had kept her word ... she had done what she'd promised she would do, bring us safely across the continent.

I touched the controls, began to turn us back and down to land.

Wait.

I waited while for reasons she did not speak, she watched westward:

Part of the earth and part of the sea, is Puff. Part of both is thee and

me, as well, I thought, we've chosen a playground suitably vast to be the stage for our lessons and adventures as mortals, our gentle games of life and death.

CHAPTER 47

Coasting

Τ he Oregon coast is where you go when you are tired tired tired of navigating. To go south, they say, keep the blue half of the world on your right.

To go north, however: that's the problem I had to figure out this morning, and what I'm going to try is this—I plan to keep the blue part on the left, and see what happens.

(A few hours have passed.)

There was an odd feeling, earlier, as I wrote the words "I plan ... ," as though I was being reminded about schemes and mice again, plus the meaning of "ganging aft agley."

No problem with the morning, except the winds were 25 knots gusting 33 a few miles north, blowing directly on our noses, and forecast stronger as the day warmed. Our speed over the ground would be around 30 mph. Dan calls these "fortuitous headwinds," since they mean more flying time for him than would a tailwind.

We reached the airport, made ready to fly, and before I even got to the Tail Section Inspection in my preflight checklist, Dan said, "Looks like you have a flat tire."

It did look that way, tailwheel all squashed against the ground, and I flickered back to the odd warning about humans planning things.

We couldn't fix the tire in Bandon. We did find a lawnmower wheel at the hardware store, which wheel fit perfectly in place of Puff's tailwheel. By the time the job was finished it was nearly noon and the wind had picked up a fair amount ... Puff's airspeed indicator bounced up to 29 mph as she sat on the ground, even before I started her engine.

Soon as I did, she made it clear that she was not in favor of a lawnmower tire for her tailwheel.

It's an emergency, Puff! We'll repair your tire at the next stop, I promise ... the tire only needs to last for one flight!

I feel so silly.

I promise ... next airport.

My promises mean something to her, now. I didn't mention this earlier, but last flight her oil was a little low and I told her I would add some before she flew again. When I checked the oil today it was lower but still within limits for flying. Pouring oil in a 20-mph wind while balancing atop the rear fuselage to reach the engine I'd rather not do, but I had promised. Yes the wind blew oil all over the place for a while, and I wiped most of it up afterward. Some of it up, anyway.

Puff noticed the fresh oil, when her engine started. After the comment about the tire she said no more, trusted me to keep my word.

I was leader again, so decided that if our groundspeed dropped to nothing I would change course and set sail for central Oregon, where the winds promised to be not quite so hurriquesque.

Blue side left, blue side left, I repeated as I brought Puff awake. She was happy with that at once, for she's been dreaming, I think, of her own hangar and of exploring new flying-grounds.

Jennifer and Puff taxied carefully in the wind, not to be blown over by the gusts, and in a minute, in position for takeoff at the end of the runway, pointed into the wind, Dan nodded to me: I'm ready to go.

I pushed the throttle ahead and Puff was flying in five seconds, pitching and yawing in the tumbling air. We turned for the beach, settled down a few feet above its runway of sand, a hundred miles long.

The air was in a hurry to get south, and it intended to take the sea along with it. Four and five rows of tall waves, all of them breaking at once onto the wide sand that's the West Coast. Just above the waterline, where the sand's still dark, one can land there safely … the moisture binds the grains, firms them.

Our groundspeed was down to 50 mph, 45 in the gusts. Deserted beach, easy landing, save for the wind it would have been a lovely soaring flight northward. Yet the wind kept battering at us, slamming our wings so they banked left and right, usually shallow sometimes steep. This, I decided at last, pushing the throttle to climb power, this is a No.

We lifted skyward, borne on rocky updrafts, till we leveled at 4,000 feet and turned inland toward calm air. Mountains below again but not for long, melting as they did into the Willamette Valley, that broad plain the color of warm grass, stretching past the horizon.

Puff didn't breathe a word about her goofy tailwheel as we taxied in for fuel, then to the tiedown spot, she and Jennifer side by side. She didn't need to, as Puff and my conscience have adjoining rooms.

An hour in the big fixed-base hangar at Corvallis and her own tailwheel tire was repaired good as new, installed again, the lawnmower wheel whisked out of sight.

You may ask how I replaced the tailwheel without a jack to lift the tail, and that is a good question. The answer is that I didn't need a jack because I had a Dan, who said he was happy to dead-lift the 160-pounds required to get the wheel off the ground so I could quick-swap it out for the lawnmower tire. I trust, should ever I need to lift the airplane again, there will be a geologist nearby.

This was a day of little flying and lots of messing around with mechanical stuff, not so touching and moving as flight. I was accepting the belief that I may be a little tired this evening as I checked into the hotel.

Hungry, though, Dan and I repaired to a Corvallis restaurant for our one meal of the day.

Entering, this is what we saw on the wall:

The sight stopped me in my tracks. How many signs do I need, how many feathers in one flight, somebody's caring over us?

I asked the waitress. "Would you mind telling me what the feather on the wall stands for?"

She glanced in that direction. "It's supposed to be a palm leaf," she said.

I ask you: if you found that figure on the wall of your restaurant, would you ask Would you mind telling me what the palm-leaf on the wall stands for?

I wouldn't. I'd say why are blue feathers following me all across the country?

A sweet little sign, but ambiguous, I thought after a while, as it wasn't meant to be a feather. The sign-leavers need to be clear, talking with their mortals, or we won't notice we're being watched over at all.

I went to my room, tossed stuff where it was convenient, dropped my room key-card on the nightstand. Only then did I notice that it had shifted part-way out of its envelope, two words visible:

(Honest, it's a photo of the cards just as I dropped them on the night-stand.)

The day snapped back into perspective. Not things that matter, Richard. It's the meaning of things.

Thank you, Granma.

CHAPTER *48*

Repair It, or Fly On?

efore one flies one's airplane, one looks it over, more or less carefully. It's called a preflight inspection, commonly a "preflight." Such things as, "Looks like you have a flat tire," those are preflight issues that need to be attended to before one goes flying.

Every aircraft has its own list of, they're not weak points, they're places to which its pilot pays special attention. Fly big jet transports, you want to be sure nobody's left a toolbox in the engine air intake, fly little airplanes you want to be sure to remove the tiedown chains before you taxi for takeoff, or try to.

The SeaRey, being in your Experimental Amateur-Built category, has a fair number of points her pilot wants to check on the preflight. When I noticed that unlike most pilots Dan takes his time, that he inspects carefully, I was curious and asked why.

His answer slowed my preflight considerably. With her propeller mounted behind the engine instead of in front, it means that whatever little nut or bolt comes loose from the engine in flight doesn't just fall harmlessly in the wilderness, it goes through the propeller. When those blades are rotating not so far below the speed of sound, collisions with hard things are not to be desired.

Thus it was, having listened, that I noticed that not one but two safety-wires had broken on Puff's engine, wires to keep exhaust-system springs from flying through the propeller should they break.

I don't mean to get way technical, but there's a point. While I replaced the broken wires, Dan was curious to know why Jennifer's engine used more fuel than Puff's. He took that extra time to track it down, and found that her engine-driven fuel pump was leaking.

He wouldn't have found that had I not found my broken wires. Coincidence speaking. What to do about it? Order a fuel pump and wait for it?

But hey, that pump has been leaking for days, and no notice from Jennifer's engine but she's using a little more fuel than usual.

Decision: Fly on!

Reckless? We didn't think so. The question we ask in decisions like this: What's the worst thing that could happen?

The fuel pump could fail completely. If it did, there's an electric backup fuel pump in the system, for just that event. If the main fuel pump stops working, the backup will keep the engine running indefinitely.

And the main hasn't failed, it's just pumping a few drops of fuel overboard.

Fly on we did, Puff in the lead because this was becoming home country to me, I've flown here before.

Travels with *Puff*

We didn't quite cross the Columbia River, we flew down its centerline for a few miles, till there on the Washington side was a long sand beach, deserted in the morning sun.

"Wheels up for the water," I called.

"Two."

I checked the river for floating logs, branches, debris of the sort one finds in rivers after heavy rains. There had not been heavy rains.

Puff touched down on the river, taxied to the beach, lowered her wheels, tried the sand. Sure, and it was firm, so Puff

the seaplane lifted out of the water and became Puff the land-plane, parked on a beach, Jennifer right behind.

With both engines shut down all we could hear were the faintest ripples of water while the river slid softly by.

We felt like Tom Sawyer and Huck Finn once more, drifted west.

The sand was warm and dry, we stayed a bit, closed our eyes for a while, as the sun had said, "Enjoy."

Then, having determined that this beach, as every other place we had landed, would likely be there to return to, we were on our way again, turning our land-planes back to seaplanes.

If I've learned one lesson in all my days, it's this: *We don't learn one lesson in all our days. We learn vast numbers of lessons, each a lone pixel. Yet the pixels come together, show our world of appearances not so blind and uncaring as it looks, a stage of shape-shifting seems-to-be on which we undestroyable spirits play in our dramas, pretending we're mortal. The lessons together: We live, each of us, beyond space and time. Mortality's a fine drama, and sweeter for remembering who we are, beyond the parts we play.*

Flying north over the emerald valley, the first blue glimmer of Puget Sound ahead, I looked to Jennifer, floating in the air alongside, watched Dan lift his camera into the wind above the cockpit, catching Puff and the water.

These two tiny seaplanes and us, what a flight we've made together! Fears and dangers and tests, along the way, ten thousand ways we could have crashed and burned in some desolate place. Yet we brought confidence along with us, what skills we had, more than a splash of devil-may-care. And trust. Dan's trust in Jennifer, my trust in Puff.

And mine in you. After that first week. The first week, your training, I thought …

You thought what, Puff?

… that our chance of surviving may have been less than … less than certain.

Oh, my, I thought: Puff has learned to be diplomatic!

She's right, though. We're free to go miserable, I thought, to wreck our lives with negative choices. We're free to live average lives on average decisions. We're free to custom-build our lives with unusual choices, on wild creative decisions. We can do all of these, if we want, in one lifetime.

Who's to stop us?

CHAPTER 49

Unknowns,
and the Confident

O ver the water northbound still, and all at once the scenery changed:
See that streak of blue behind the Space Needle? That's Lake
Union, hub for Kenmore Air, the biggest seaplane airline in the country.
I thought Puff might like to touch down there, blink at the city for a
minute or two, remind her to cherish that she's a country girl.

Just for a minute, then we were off again, upSound, toward the San Juan Islands.

The sea was as calm as ever I've seen it, welcome-wagon for the new young lady, moved in up the street.

One last radio call, "Three Four Six Papa Echo, flight of two, five miles south for a straight-in Runway Three-Four."

Then Puff whispered down, feather-light, to touch first time a runway she'll come to know well.

Repair it, or fly on? So often, flying-on's the choice. Wait for repair, for every detail to be perfect, one may never get off the ground. Might as well take off, and if it has to be fixed, fix it along the way! That advice can get us in a lot of trouble, and it can set us free.

I felt that Puff was impressed, taxiing in. *The biggest hangar on the field, it's mine?*

It is. Fifty-nine stops, coast to coast, 62 hours flying. Now we're home.

Pleasure, then sudden alarm.

But I'm not going to stay on the ground, am I? Our trip isn't over, we'll be flying every day?

Hangars are warm refuge for the pause between flights, Puff, comfortable shelters for rest and repair. They're no place to live when we're ready to fly.

I'm ready.

Soon as we wash away the sand and dust and travel-streaks from the flying so far, the next voyage begins: lakes and islands you've never seen, bright water you've never touched before!

And Jennifer?

Jennifer and Dan are staying for a while, we're off together soon to points unknown.

Points unknown!

Something in that sound, thrilled her.

How she's grown! Puff loves her unknowns, now, flying confident toward each, and a little devil-may-care.

Would you believe? In that very moment, our two seaplanes stopped at the hangar, the roar of an engine overhead, sudden-blasting, wheels slam-bounced on the rooftop: flash of a wave and a shout,

"HI-HO DOWN THERE! *I'M FREEDOM-BOUND!*"

It's Toad in his Aero-Plane, away for the horizon.

Wait up, Toad! We're coming too!